MW01449305

GRATITUDE

To my husband, Joseph Cole, thank you for being there for me and with me every step of this journey.

To my daddy, Kenneth Johnson, I am because of you and mom. Thank you for living the sermons you preach and for showing Troy, Bryan, and I how to live out John 15:5.

To my brothers, sisters-in-love, wonderful family, supportive circle of friends who keep me encouraged and iron-sharpened, mentors that share so selflessly, Sorors of Delta Sigma Theta Sorority, Inc. and The Quad, I love you!

To Marshawn and Jack, I love you like family. Thank you for helping me see new dimensions and teaching me to believe bigger. #godfidence

To my dream team, who have helped bring my dream of being an author to life, we did it! Patty, Tia, Joel, Brittany, Drea, Justin, Kelly, Tanika, Lizzy, Andrew, Blake, Brenda, Leah, Adam, thank you so much!

" But seek first the kingdom of God and his righteousness, and all these things will be added to you." - Matthew 6:33

THRIVE Through IT

A Guide to Help You Redefine Resilience, Communicate with Empathy, and Practice Allyship in Your Life and Business

BRITTANY N. COLE

Copyright © 2020 by Brittany N. Cole

All rights reserved. No part of this publication may be reproduced, stored in a retrieval system, stored in a database and/or published in any form or by any means, electronic, mechanical, photocopying, recording, or otherwise, without the prior written permission of the publisher

Some of the names and personal characteristics of individuals involved have been changed to disguise their identities. Any resulting resemblance is entirely unintentional.
Published in the United States by Career Thrivers, LLC.
Careerthrivers.com
For more information about bulk purchases, please contact Career Thrivers via email at info@careerthrivers.com.

Career Thrivers and The Resilience Roadmap are registered trademarks of Brittany N. Cole. For more information and free resources, please visit Brittanyncole.com

Scripture quotations are taken from THE MESSAGE, copyright © 1993, 2002, 2018 by Eugene H. Peterson. Used by permission of NavPress. All rights reserved. Represented by Tyndale House Publishers, Inc.

Library of Congress Cataloging-in-Publication Data is available upon request.
EBook ISBN: 978-1-7354747-0-0
Hardback ISBN: 978-1-7354747-8-6
Paperback ISBN: 978-1-7354747-9-3
Artwork and Book design by Patty McAvoy Designs

Dedicated to my first example of what it looks like to THRIVE Through It, my first best friend, my mom, **LaBrenda Sonette Johnson**.

I'm forever grateful for your lived lessons on how to thrive through the tragedies and triumphs of life.

> "My mission in life is not merely to survive, but to thrive; and to do so with some passion, some compassion, some humor, and some style."
>
> — *Maya Angelou*

TABLE OF CONTENTS

GRIEF

1.	What is Resilience? Really?	19
2.	Career Grief When No One Died	36

GRIT

3.	Survival Mode Isn't Sustainable	70
4.	Don't Should Yourself	88
5.	Communicating with Empathy	112

GRACE

6.	Manage Your Mindset	146
7.	Self-Care Is Resilience	171
8.	Supporting Others Through It	195
9.	Proceed with Grace	248
10.	Gratitude	265

BRITTANY N. COLE — THRIVE THROUGH IT

The Resilience Roadmap®

GRIEF

01. ACKNOWLEDGE THE FEELINGS
02. IDENTIFY THE LOSS

GRIT

03. REVEAL AND DEAL TO HEAL
04. BE OKAY BEING UNCOMFORTABLE
05. HAVE THE TOUGH CONVERSATIONS

GRACE

06. REIMAGINE TO REINVENT THE NOW YOU
07. BE WHAT YOU NEED
08. SHARE THE LOAD
09. FOCUS FOWARD

FORWARD

Brittany is known by many in many different ways. She is a coach of coaches, a leader of leaders, a master motivator, a persistent prayer partner, a corporate consultant, a selfless sorority sister, a dedicated daughter, and many more. Some know her as an auntie, sister, friend, business leader, mentor, former personal stylist, or even by the high school nickname, "BJ." But I have the exclusive honor of knowing her as my wife.

Our friendship started in high school in 5th-period art class, where Brittany (whose last name was Johnson) decided to sit at the "C" table with me (last name Cole). Our friendship flourished over AOL Instant Messenger, where "ynattirb" (her name backwards) and "BlackLuv3001" (me, of course) would have hours-long conversations about everything and nothing all at the same time.

While it feels like our deep friendship just started yesterday, I have had the blessing of knowing Brittany in multiple capacities for nearly twenty years. In two decades of witnessing my wife and friend change, grow, and ultimately evolve into the thought-leader she currently is, a few things have always remained constant:

Her "passion for fashion." Brittany has always had great style. You will not find anyone that dresses as fly as my wife. The walking embodiment of "you look good, you feel good," each day, I have seen her dress in a flair that is unique to her and loved by the rest of us.

Her work ethic is unmatched. She loves working hard and can work around the clock. At times, working is her form of leisure. If you have ever worked, partnered, or served with her, I am sure you have received an email from her in the early morning regarding some task she is working to improve.

She is a natural-born leader. I can name countless instances where I have seen Brittany step into a leadership role, formally and informally, to execute with precision. It is just her nature to see a problem and step up to inspire people around a solution.

She is a master communicator and teacher. Communication and teaching are her God-given gifts. I have witnessed Brittany work on a course or talk in her office for weeks, writing her outline on her whiteboard and creating slides to bring the main talking points to life. I've even watched her prepare for a TEDx talk with very short notice and, in three days literally, walk on the stage as if she's practiced for months and give a jaw-dropping, thought-provoking, awe-inspiring speech. Some people just have "it." And her "it" is teaching and speaking.

She has a passion for giving back. Brittany relentlessly gives without a self-centered motive. I have witnessed her give money to others anonymously on many occasions. From buying groceries for mothers in need, buying kids much-needed winter jackets, buying young ladies' dresses to attend formals, or even covering the course and coaching for women she mentors. Brittany has a heart for pouring into others. I think this comes from her observation of her mother over the years, who helped others at all costs.

She is resourceful and relentless. If you give Brittany a task, you can rest assure she will complete it exceptionally well. She does not believe in only meeting the minimum requirements. She goes over and beyond, whether for work, church, business, friends, or family.

Despite the amazing qualities she's had since high school, Brittany's rhythm and record of jumping over hurdles and pulling people up along the way all came to a halt in June 2017. She had always handled everything so well, but this grief was different. I saw sides of Brittany that I had never seen before. Her grief experience was debilitating, and in this case, she could not "dress up" to make herself feel better. She could not spend more time at work to feel better. She could not focus on mastering some new feat to make herself feel better. She had to sit with her grief. She had to understand her grief. She had to find a way to thrive through it.

While witnessing Brittany on her journey, I observed something surprising, yet inspiring. Late into the night, she would diagram her thoughts and feelings on a whiteboard and extra-large Post-it notes. At first, I thought she was "just" working through her feelings visually. But years later, I realize she was using this experience to give back to others by leading them through grief and teaching actionable ways to thrive.

It's been years of watching her navigate her grief journey and write what started as a series of blog posts. However, her earnest desire to help others experiencing grief in many different areas of life grew from a blog to this book. I am excited for you to experience her guidance through this journey. Are you ready to thrive through it?

- BlackLuv3001 aka Cool Guy at the "C Table" aka Her Husband, Joseph

A NOTE FROM BRITTANY

Have you ever taken a long road trip? I'm talking one of those long trips that's at least eight hours! Growing up, I can remember countless drives from our home in Nashville, Tennessee, to my mother's hometown of Charleston, South Carolina. My dad would be in the driver's seat, mom in the passenger, and my brother and me with our marked territory in the back. Out of all the times we drove to Charleston—sometimes through Atlanta, Georgia most of the time through Knoxville, Tennessee—one thing was always consistent, we stopped for rest breaks!

As a child, the more rest stops, the better because these breaks meant snacks, stretching, and my mom and I would request the occasional rest break at our favorite "on the way" TJ Maxx or Marshalls to shop! Isn't it interesting how we relish in rest stops on long trips as a child, but as we get older, we prioritize the speed of getting to the destination over the joy along the journey

As an adult, my preferences for long trips have changed. Many of us see pit stops as prolonging our trip. We're often so rushed to get where we're going that even the thought of stopping frustrates us. However, the fact of the matter is that if you're taking a long trip, whether you want to stop or not, rest stops are necessary. As I reminisce, the rest stops made the journey that much more memorable!

I believe this is also true of our journey through living with loss. When we lose something or someone important to us, it's a very long road. Can you imagine going on a twelve-hour road trip, at night, with no map or GPS, in the car alone without stopping? This is how many of us journey through loss—alone, without a guide, and pretending that we can power through without ever stopping. I believe it's the rest stops that help us to re-energize, re-focus, and re-calibrate—enabling us to make the journey in a more meaningful way.

In the summer of 2017, I started writing a blog at labrendajohnson.com. Eventually that blog led me to write a book. The strange part was I had already started writing a slightly different book—a much more comfortable one. A "strategic" book where I was sharing how to advance your career. I had the outline fully mapped out with a framework for how to navigate your career, and strengthen your skills in networking, emotional intelligence, communicating, storytelling, personal branding, managing up, etc. I had tips for all the topics. This was the book I wanted to share. The comfortable, strategic, and well-aligned resource with a companion curriculum for our inclusive leadership development firm, Career Thrivers.

However, I was led to write about resilience. Who wants to read a book about grief, loss and adversity? How will this fit into my pretty business plan? Literally every time I tried to pick up the career book, I had this overwhelming feeling that this wasn't what I was supposed to be writing. So, I started writing "the grief book" begrudgingly at first. But it has become the most beautiful experience and has helped me through my own grief journey. I've been sharing this redefined perspective on resilience as a speaker while I've been writing this book. It has helped me see that this message is so needed, **especially at a time where we're faced with loss connected to the dual pandemics of covid and racism.**

Still, it was hard to write this book. Have you ever had the kind of experience where you're being stretched beyond where you've been before, and at the same time you know it's necessary? I wrote this book (the second time around ☺) with you in mind. You're a high achiever and likely in a place where you're leading and looked to for your performance, perspective, and influence on people. To everyone else, you've got it all together. You're "so strong" and an "inspiration." Yes, and at the same time you know what it's like to suffer in silence.

You have increasing responsibilities and expectations while also navigating the increasing weight of grief. The weight of change, transition, and loss is heavy, and you want to be "resilient" and also real about where you are and what you need to not just get over it, but grow through it. I can relate to this experience and thought that I could press my foot on the gas to "power through" the pain. I was **trying to compartmentalize my life, but the reality was: my grief was showing.** The truth is, we bring all of who we are—our beliefs, our values, our experiences, and yes even our grief—to every space we're in.

Every space includes the workplace. Much of the discomfort we feel when we're met with change, challenges or loss is grief. I want to help us take the rest stop and unpack our feelings, communicate our emotions, and thrive from a place of courage and vulnerability. If you've experienced this or are in this place right now, I want you to know that you can acknowledge grief in your life— career grief, personal grief, and the collective grief of a global pandemic and racial injustice. You can acknowledge it and journey through it in an authentic and intentional way. This is exactly why I've written this book and created The Resilience Roadmap® to help us do just that! To get your own copy of The Resilience Roadmap® and other resources, be sure to get your free gift – the Thrive Through It Toolkit – at brittanyncole.com/book.

As you read this book and consider your resilience journey, I hope you will take the time to S.T.O.P. along the way to do a few things:

SIT STILL – Find a space where you can quiet your mind and focus. Take some deep breaths to exhale any worry, doubt, or judgment. You're worth taking a moment to yourself to stop and get still.

THINK IT THROUGH – Ask yourself these questions: How do I feel about this? What do I think about how I feel? What is my best next step?

OPENLY OBSERVE – Notice your body language, thoughts, feelings, and emotions and get them out. Write, type, or talk out your observations. As you're getting them out don't judge them. Observe them. There is no right or wrong here.

PROCEED WITH PURPOSE – Plan how you want to proceed. Now that you've taken the time to stop and become more self-aware, what's your next best step? You don't have to have everything figured out, but consider how you want to proceed with intention and purpose.

These stops aren't a waste of time. In time they will help you become more efficient with the time you have and more effective in how you lead other people. I'm excited to take this journey with you as we redefine resilience with a roadmap that helps us stop to thrive through with purpose. I'm rooting for you!

LET'S THRIVE TOGETHER,

Brittany N. Cole

SECTION ONE

GRIEF

"You don't have to experience grief, but you can only avoid it by avoiding love. Love and grief are inextricably intertwined."

— DAVID KESSLER,
FINDING MEANING: THE SIXTH STAGE OF GRIEF

CHAPTER 1
What Is Resilience? Really?

Everyone is bouncing back but me

It was Sunday night, June 4, 2017, and we were on the phone. I was lying in bed listening to her cheer on the Cleveland Cavaliers for the NBA playoff game. I can remember telling her to calm down because she was getting so excited about how well LeBron James was playing. I'm not sure I know a more intense person to watch basketball, football, or any sports event with. "Woo! Go, LeBron!" She was yelling at the television and through the phone while simultaneously talking to me in between plays. I was watching the game too on YouTube TV from my iPad, lying in bed in our one-bedroom apartment in the middle of Manhattan. (We'd recently moved to New York from Chattanooga, TN and hit the ground running with work, so we hadn't set up cable service just yet). Isn't there something special about watching the same thing on the phone with someone you care about at the same time, in different places?

It almost felt like I was right on the couch with her. We were watching the game together—from Nashville to New York. She jokingly asked me about the guest in our apartment. We had seen a mouse in our second-floor walk-up on 71st and 2nd, and I was ready to pack up and move ASAP! This was my first time living outside of Tennessee, and I was so over this first apartment experience! I told her we hadn't caught the mouse yet. She reassured me that it would be just fine and that a mouse getting in could happen anywhere. I appreciated her attempt at reassuring me that this visitor had nothing to do with New York itself or the old walk-up apartment building where we lived. "Mmmm hm, yeah, okay," I thought to myself.

She always tried to make sure I felt reassured in any situation, that despite what was happening at the moment, things would still work out. I shared that we were approved to move into a new apartment in a full-service, doorman building in a couple of weeks, and I couldn't wait to move! She was happy to hear that we had found an apartment we liked and said, as she usually did those first few months of our big move, "I'll be up there to visit this summer!" I said okay, with the excited expectation that we'd be hitting museums, great restaurants, and all the great festivals and boutiques in a couple of short months, just like our first girls' trip to NYC! Only this time, I lived there!

Her health continued to improve, and she was getting stronger and sounded good while watching this game. The next day I had a big meeting, so I knew that I would be out like a light for the night as soon as we finished talking. She filled me in on the great weekend she had. She was feeling so much better, and her childhood best friend from her hometown of Charleston, South Carolina, came to town to visit and brought her daughter. We had always taken girls' trips together every year since middle school. This trip was planned with a quick turnaround, and I had already purchased a flight to be in Nashville the following weekend. So, I was going back and forth about joining in on the fun this time. I decided to miss out this time, stick with my plan to see my mom the next weekend, and surely we would be back to our regularly scheduled girls' trips soon!

She shared how wonderful it was to get to go back to church that morning and how excited and encouraged everyone was to see her. It was the first Sunday, and she gave a stirring testimony about how the Lord was healing her. I could hear her smiling through the phone. She asked about Joe before getting off the phone and told me to tell him she loves him. We said our goodnights, and that was the last time I spoke to my mother.

A NEW LENS ON GRIEF

The first time my paradigm on grief shifted was the year before my mother's death. Joe and I were sitting in a small group Bible study on a cold Wednesday evening in 2016. We had been married a little more than a year, so it seemed right to attend the For Married Women and For Married Men small group. We signed up and were assigned the accompanying two books by Tony Evans. This amazing married couple that we love facilitated the six-week session for our small group. Some couples in the group were married ten, fifteen, and twenty-plus years. As newlyweds who spent the first year of marriage long distance between grad school and climbing the corporate ladder (more on that later), we were hungry for examples and guidance to get through what had been a tough year.

We were about halfway through the class, and Mrs. Creech began to share the story of her transition to a new city and having to leave a job she loved, working in her career field. She described the feelings of leaving the familiar city, having to quit her job and relocate her family to a new place she knew nothing about to follow her husband's career. "I was grieving," she explained. At that moment, I realized that much of what I was experiencing and feeling in that first year of marriage, navigating ambiguity, and transition in my personal life and professional career, was grief. I'd never connected my emotions about the life and career changes that were happening to grief. As I listened to Mrs. Creech share her story, I realized I was grieving.

WHAT IS GRIEF?

Most of the time we associate grief with the death of a loved one. When we think of grief, we typically think of our own experience losing a close friend or family member or the experience of someone we know grieving the death of a loved one. The ending of life can trigger many emotions that we often tie a bow around as grief. This idea that grief is the sorrow that results only from physical death keeps many of us from recognizing moments in our lives when we grieve other kinds of loss. I've learned throughout my journey that in actuality, grief can present very differently than the box we usually place it in.

> *This idea that grief is the sorrow that results only from physical death keeps many of us from recognizing moments in our lives when we grieve other kinds of loss.*

This book is for those of us navigating the ambiguity of life experiences that leave us struggling to make sense of what to do next. That feeling of being at a crossroads due to change, challenge, or transition is the result of a loss. Before we can even begin this discussion thought, we must first discuss what exactly is grief.

My grief experiences have taught me to expand my former, narrow lens of associating grief with only the physical loss of life. Grief can cover a wide range of personal and professional life experiences and trauma. So then, what is grief? Grief is a natural emotion of complex, conflicting, and frequently unpredictable feelings in response to a loss or change that disrupts a familiar pattern or prevents the desired outcome. Let's look at each section of our definition a bit more closely:

> *Grief is a natural emotion of complex, conflicting, and frequently unpredictable feelings in response to a loss or change that disrupts a familiar pattern or prevents the desired outcome.*

Grief is very much a **natural emotion**. It is normal to respond to loss with overwhelming feeling. However, we often feel the need to mask and bottle up our natural, emotional response. It's essential to be mindful that the loss's impact will vary depending on our background, perspective, belief, personality, and context. The greater the loss is for us, the more overwhelming the emotion. Most would agree that the loss of people and opportunities we invest in and value the most will trigger the most gripping emotion. However, it is crucial also to be mindful that even losses which don't directly impact us – such as the collective grief of a thought leader or publicly viewed murder of someone we identify with – can trigger grief's natural feeling.

Recognizing these emotions are natural is one thing; normalizing them can sometimes be another story. Although we may want to maintain a positive and optimistic perspective on life's challenges, it is critical not to let that keep us from acknowledging and experiencing grief's natural emotions. Do not allow someone else's arbitrary expectations and timing to place a muzzle on your process. Most of us have heard the saying, "Everyone grieves differently." However, I have also found that people are swift to pass judgment on how long others "should" experience the natural and normal emotions that come with grief.

Grief will cause **complex, conflicting, and often unpredictable feelings.** This characteristic of our definition of grief has been one of the most challenging aspects of my grief process. The conflict is trying to balance the intense emotions of sadness, anger, emptiness, and even regret while also having the opposite feelings of gratitude, joy, hope, laughter, and even relief. This tug-of-war can seem endless and leave you feeling like you are fighting a losing battle.

One of the reasons I believe this message is important to share is so that we shift to having a more comprehensive perspective on grief. It can be very challenging to take the time to address these feelings, especially as leaders. When we face adversity and loss, many will tell you things will get better with time. I don't believe that; things get better as you are wise with how you spend the time you have. Time doesn't heal us on its own, but people that deal with their grief over time will heal. This time is best spent being honest, transparent, reflective, and committed to your resilience road—not merely so that you bounce back—but instead to lead you forward to reimagine your life and business in new ways.

The conflicting feelings of grief is an area that has been very hard for me to manage. As someone with a laid-back, even-tempered personality who is very poised under pressure, the feeling of being out of control emotionally has in and of itself been a wholly different and overwhelming experience. Again, it's important to remind ourselves that these are very normal and natural responses to any loss—such as those that happen in our career, personal life, business, or relationships. When I've found myself feeling these intense, conflicting feelings, it's been helpful to spend some time in introspection, honestly evaluating what these feelings are **in response to.**

Your initial response to this question will feel obvious, but I encourage you to dig deeper. For example, my initial response would be, "I'm feeling this pain because my mother died." This causal relationship seems obvious. That's what I was telling myself. However, when I sat down and was honest and in prayer about what exactly I was responding to, there were pain points much deeper and intertwined in the experience of losing my mother. Guilt, anger, and regret were some of those hidden triggers I was also responding to. These are the areas I've had to unpack because it was only when I dealt with the roots of my grief that I've been able to begin healing and moving forward with real resilience.

The roots are those buried parts of grief others don't see and the areas that can be easy for you to pretend aren't there. You know, when it's more vital for you to appear to have "bounced back" so people applaud how "strong you are" rather than journeying through the guilt connected to your grief. The roots are often found in the nuances around your loss, the dynamics that were less than perfect; the people who were or weren't there; the words you did or didn't say; the time you did or didn't have, etc. These aspects can make the gripping nature of grief nearly suffocating. What are you grieving in response to? What are those deep roots around your loss that need to be uprooted, assessed, and addressed?

> *The roots are those buried parts of grief others don't see and the areas that can be easy for you to pretend aren't there.*

Let's examine the last two sections of our definition. Grief is a loss or change that disrupts a familiar pattern, ends a relationship, or prevents the desired outcome. This is the part of our description that speaks to how common grief is. In addition to the recognizable loss of a loved one's empty seat around the holidays, there are experiences we all share within our families, careers, business, and relationships that have disrupted our patterns or prevented the desired outcome. Whether they are perceived as negative experiences such as a divorce or layoff, or positive experiences such as having a new baby or

> *...loss or change that disrupts a familiar pattern, ends a relationship, or prevents the desired outcome...*

relocating for a promotion, these examples can all catapult us into feelings of grief.

From books like this to websites to small groups, many resources can help you along your journey. Sometimes the best help we can receive, though, is spending time with ourselves in honest introspection. That means being self-aware when we are grieving, identifying the source of these emotions, and gathering the resources and tools we need to navigate the crossroads we're experiencing.

GETTING REAL ABOUT RESILIENCE

What comes to mind when you hear the word resilience?
Perseverance?
Flexibility?
Overcoming obstacles?
Succeeding despite the challenges?
Adaptability?
Fortitude?

I believe all of these are aspects of what it means to be resilient. In addition to this list, we often hear the phrase "ability to bounce back" associated with resilience. Picture a pile of rubber bands. Imagine you're holding a rubber band, stretched out between both of your index fingers. It's stretched out far. You can see the elastic cracking. What would happen if you moved one of your fingers, letting go of the rubber band, and it bounced back? Ouch, right? That pop against your hand would hurt!

This is how many of us approach resilience. We prioritize how quickly we can bounce back, even despite being stretched to the point we almost crack—not recognizing the sting that comes with prioritizing bounce back expeditiously despite the loss we've encountered.

To thrive through loss, we must get real about resilience. Let's redefine and reframe how we think about resilience by getting R.E.A.L. Language is a powerful tool. If we allow ourselves to be entirely honest about our experiences with grief and loss, we'd probably agree that grief changes us. We don't bounce back. Resilience is about our ability to thrive through loss, extrapolating the lessons from our experiences to journey forward with not only grit but also grace. Here are four key areas to help us get R.E.A.L. as we redefine RESILIENCE:

> *To thrive through loss... we must get real about resilience.*

> *Resilience is about our ability to thrive through loss, extrapolating the lessons from our experiences to journey forward with not only grit but also grace.*

R.E.A.L. RESILIENCE

1. **REFLECT** – How are you making space to express how you feel? We have to be reflective. Taking the time to sit down and ask ourselves, "How am I feeling as a result of losing _____" is an essential first step. What specifically did you lose? We have to identify the actual loss. When we're so focused on bouncing back, we often skip this step to "get over it" or distract ourselves with tasks, work, etc. Taking the time to get clear on the source of our pain, disappointment, or trauma is critical to thriving through. This process has helped me identify the root cause of my pain, particularly in moments of a lost opportunity, job, or experience. It's important to note that "fine" is not a feeling. As you're reflecting, utilize "The Wheel of Emotions" of "The Feeling Wheel" below which was first developed by American Psychologist Robert Plutchik in 1980 to help you name your feelings. There are several variations of this wheel, but essentially this visual represents eight primary emotions (joy, sadness, acceptance, disgust, fear, anger, surprise and anticipation), which Plutchik believed were the foundations of all other emotions.[1]

---

[1] Berlinsky Schine, Laura. How to Check in With Yourself Using an Emotion Wheel. Fairygodboss. https://fairygodboss.com/career-topics/emotion-wheel

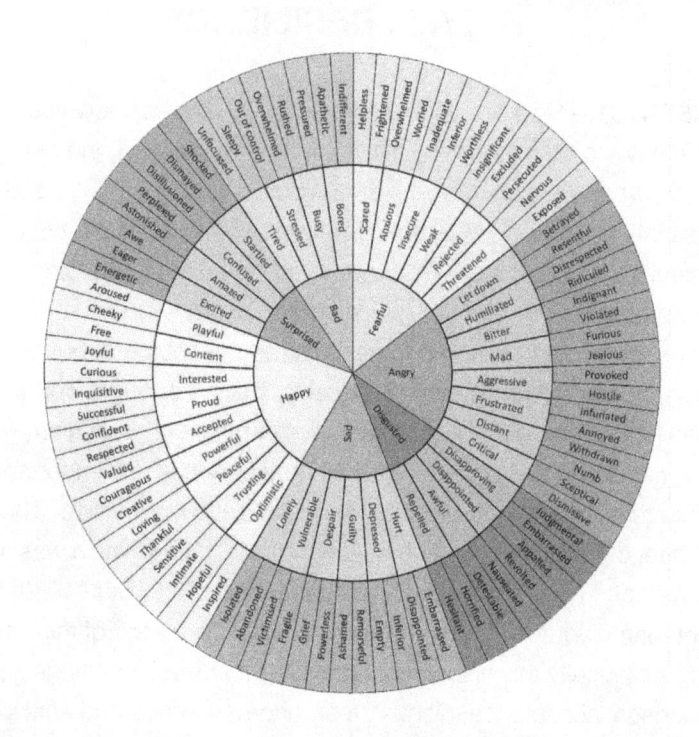

2. **EVALUATE** – As we're reflecting and identifying what we've lost, next it's essential to ask, "How is this impacting me?" What changes have you or will you make as a result of the loss? What conversations do you need to have to gain more clarity? Who do you need to have a crucial conversation with to be more transparent? Evaluating where you are while also anticipating the potential disruption due to this loss is an integral part of redefining resilience. Often, we harness the tools and information we need for the next steps in this evaluation phase.

3. **ADJUST** – Where do you need to make adjustments? This step involves accepting the outcome and also determining a new or next action. When we skip to this step without the first two, it often leaves us making ill-informed decisions or taking action that isn't productive. Instead of dismissing or diminishing what we've experienced, we can embrace going and growing through what we've lost to journey forward with courage, purpose, authenticity, and joy.

4. **LOSE THE CAPE** – This is where grace comes in. As a woman whose career has been shaped by being the only in many rooms in corporate America, I understand what it's like to feel the need to be impenetrable by circumstances, bias, or even ill-equipped leaders. This cape of protection and sign of strength sometimes creates a lack of vulnerability, especially in the workplace. I now believe that resilience requires vulnerability and sharing the load to thrive through loss in a meaningful way. It's okay to be real about where you are. Losing the cape helps you model a level of transparency and authenticity that become powerful for healing.

Thriving through grief, change, and challenges don't happen overnight. It's not about this pseudo strength you have to project. Instead, you're being reflective by thriving through with real resilience, by evaluating where you are and who to connect with, by making the adjustments you need, and by losing the cape to share the load and be for others what you need yourself.

Self-awareness will help you reveal the root of your loss. This discovery is essential for our mental and emotional well-being. Often when grief is more obvious, people will ask how they can help you or support your transition. I discovered I could only articulate additional needs after I sat with myself to acknowledge what I felt. This introspection can take some time, so don't feel the need to get everything sorted and resolved in one sitting. Grief is a self-re-discovery process as you uncover who you are in your new set of circumstances. When you allow yourself the time and space to articulate what you are feeling, you're better able to guide others on how they can support you in your process—both personally and professionally.

> *Grief is a self-re-discovery process as you uncover who you are in your new set of circumstances. When you allow yourself the time and space to articulate what you are feeling, you're better able to guide others on how they can support you in your process—both personally and professionally.*

My prayer for all of us as we come to truly understand what grief means, what it looks like for us, and what circumstances beyond physical death can trigger it is that we will have gradual restoration in every facet of our lives!

G.R.I.E.F. (Gradual Restoration In Every Facet)

As I am traveling on this journey, I've seen how grief can take over every area of your life. If you let it, grief can be destructive to your health, relationships, career, finances, and most importantly, your mental wellness. As we take this journey together, I hope that you will be encouraged and equipped to experience gradual restoration in every facet of your life. **Let's do this!**

Thoughts along the journey:

1. Acknowledging The Feelings

Now that we have a more comprehensive definition of grief and we've redefined resilience, here are some questions we can ask ourselves as we STOP to spend time reflecting. I've found that grief isn't this fluid, step by step process, so I encourage you to join me and begin writing your thoughts down. You can start by using the space below to write your thoughts on paper.

Review your last twelve months, from the month and year you're reading this book, to the same month the previous year and list your losses. This exercise will require vulnerability and self-awareness, especially if you share with a friend. What loss have you experienced.

Job loss?	Termination of a friendship?
Divorce?	Changing churches?
The death of a loved one?	The old normal

_____

_____

_____

_____

_____

_____

_____

_____

_____

_____

QUESTIONS TO ASK YOURSELF:

1. How am I feeling?

2. What loss am I currently experiencing due to a change in my usual pattern? What desired outcome am I grieving?

3. What is at the root of this loss?

4. What am I feeling? What thoughts do I have that I haven't articulated?

5. In what ways have I allowed myself to mourn and grieve?

6. What do I want?

7. What are the conflicting thoughts I am having?

CHAPTER 2
Grief When No One Died
We're supposed to grin and bear this, right?

Ambition has always come naturally to me. Growing up playing sports—basketball, volleyball, track, and taking dance— tap, ballet, tumbling, and jazz meant I learned how to succeed and win. You show up, work hard, practice, stay disciplined, play to your strengths, and you'll perform well. People will love you, and you will win. Work hard, play hard, people notice your skill, and you advance. That's how sports worked, and that's the same paradigm I took into corporate America. Can you relate? Let's just say that's not how advancing in the workplace operates.

Thanks to INROADS, I started my training for the corporate games early. INROADS is a career development organization whose mission I can still recite to this day, "To develop and place talented minority youth in business and industry and prepare them for corporate and community leadership." My professional development started as a junior in high school as a participant in the pre-college component of INROADS Nashville. We would attend professional development sessions on Saturdays that included Toastmasters and SAT/ACT prep classes. As a sophomore in undergrad, I earned an internship at the coveted company every intern wanted to work for as a pharmaceutical sales rep! Not only was the pay exceptional, but the internship also came complete with a laptop, American Express card, and a company rental car for the entire summer! Essentially, we were able to drive whatever we could negotiate. It was a sweet deal! Little did I know I was heading into some of the most challenging games I've ever played.

WOMEN IN THE WORKPLACE

For the past six years, LeanIn.org and McKinsey & Co. have released the largest study on the state of women and their experiences in corporate America. Their 2019 Women in The Workplace study states that women of color aren't only significantly underrepresented, but also far less likely to be promoted from individual contributor to a manager (the "broken rung"), more likely to face daily discrimination, and less likely to receive the support of our managers.[2] As often the only Black woman in the room, these findings accurately reflect many of my experiences across twelve years in corporate America. Not only do Black women experience feelings of isolation due to a lack of belonging in many organizations, but there's also this heightened expectation from colleagues to be the sole representative for the entire race.

In this sixth year of their most recent Women in the Workplace study, the research from LeanIn.org and McKinsey cover data from 317 organizations employing more than twelve million people. The report details the impact of COVID-19 on women in the workplace. They found that "a crisis is looming" for mothers, senior-level women, and Black women—all of which face distinct challenges that could "erase all the

---

[2] Jess Huang, Alexis Krivkovich, Irina Starikova, Lareina Yee, and Delia Zanoschi, "Women in the Workplace," The State of Women in Corporate America, *2019* McKinsey & Company and LeanIn.Org *Women in the Workplace!* Accessed May 28, 2019. https://leanin.org/women-in-the-workplace-2019

progress we've made toward gender diversity in the sixth year of this study."[3] The impact of loss in 2020 for working women has one in four considering downshifting their career or leaving the workforce altogether! For these reasons and more, there's never been a more critical time to have conversations about grief and loss in the workplace and understand the variable impact on women of color. One of the best resources to understand the experiences of BIPOC (Black, Indigenous and People of Color) women in the workplace is Minda Harts' book The Memo: What Women of Color Need to Know to Secure a Seat at the Table. It's a must-read for any people leader and every working professional to understand how the data in these LeanIn/McKinsey studies are lived every day by Black and Brown women.

> *There's never been a more critical time to have conversations about grief and loss in the workplace and understand the variable impact on women of color.*

I'll never forget the mental gymnastics I experienced in a sales meeting during a year beginning meeting. For the first time, our senior leadership shared about the importance of diversity during a company-wide town hall. I was pleased to finally hear the senior leadership team talk about its diversity plan with the entire company. However, most of my teammates had the opposite response. They were confused,

---

[3] Rachel Thomas and Marianne Cooper, Ph.D, et. al. "Women in the Workplace," The State of Women in Corporate America, *2020* McKinsey & Company and LeanIn.Org *Women in the Workplace*/ Accessed September 10, 2020. https://leanin.org/women-in-the-workplace-2020

frustrated, and disagreed with the company placing a priority on diversity and inclusion. As the youngest and only Black woman on my team, I could feel my body heat up and my jaw clench in response to what I was hearing.

The team meeting turned into a debate about the focus on diversity as being unfair. I remember monitoring my facial expressions and, in my head, saying, "keep your brows straight, Brittany. Don't frown. Listen to at least three colleagues first before you share." It was apparent the entire room was waiting on me to speak when our manager finally asked me (and only me) directly what my thoughts were on the topic. I proceeded to tactfully share my thoughts in a measured way about why diversity isn't unfair, how it improves business outcomes and why it doesn't mean white men won't get the job because a woman or black person is also applying. I'll never forget the way I had to run outside of myself and grab myself before reacting versus responding to this last line. In hindsight, I appreciated that my manager even made room in the meeting to have the conversation. It made it very clear who I was working with, and the chasm of diversity, inclusion, and equity learning and development needed at every level of the organization.

CAREER AND IDENTITY

Our career is often the source of frustration, anxiety, stress, and disappointment in our lives. Often, we find ourselves at the crossroads of some of the most significant decisions that will impact every area of our life due to deciding which career path to take. We don't even recognize how we allow our careers to be the axis and focal point that the rest of our lives revolve around.

I decided not to go directly to law school and moved back to Nashville after graduating from undergrad from the University of Tennessee, Knoxville, in Political Science and Communications. After my INROADS internship, I accepted a job offer in Nashville. When I thought about advancing my career, I knew I'd had a competitive advantage thanks to my INROADS experience and internship. An intentional focus on diversity, equity, and inclusion has always been part of my career journey.

Working smart, enjoying my career, and leading people to elevate and achieve more was my vision of success. From the early days as an intern, I knew my ultimate job would be about leading a team of people to accomplish extraordinary goals and dreams they hadn't seen for themselves previously. With this vision in my mind, I knew I was headed for the C-Suite and wanted to leverage every experience I could to get there.

Most of the life decisions I made early in my career were through the lens of what I wanted to experience in my career. Whether it was taking on extra projects (these would serve as part-time jobs I would work on after work) or deciding to relocate to a new city for a promotion, I quickly learned that having my career at the core of my life wasn't sustainable. I also noticed the experiences I had in my career were different from my white colleagues' experiences. My identity as a Black woman directly impacted my career experiences, every day, from colleagues to customers.

There's identity grief we don't talk about much. We say things such as "What you do isn't who you are," and although I believe that to be true, it isn't how we operate the majority of the time. Our preparation, engagement, and even responses from others often shift based on our career identity. Our career choices shape our life experiences, impact who we become, and influence many of our adult experiences. It takes real, intentional work not to allow the wave of titles and career transitions to be the center of your life decisions. So, what happens when our career shifts? What about when it shifts beyond our control? Things are going well, you performed well the previous year, you are adding value to your team, and suddenly, you're on the layoff list. What happens when we are faced with shedding an aspect of our identity that has become the lens by which others see us and hold us in high esteem? I believe that many of us, right now at this moment, are working through career grief. We've experienced the loss of who we thought we were because we've given so much to an organization that we now no longer identify with as an employee. What do you do when what you have done has become who you are known to be? How do you reimagine and reinvent?

> *Our career choices shape our life experiences, impact who we become, and influence many of our adult experiences.*

WHAT YOU DO ISN'T WHO YOU ARE, OR IS IT?

We often judge people based on their level of perceived influence relative to their career experience or title. Have you ever noticed that one of the first questions we often ask people when we meet them is, "What do you do?" Based on their response, we form a picture in our minds and often perceive their level of value in our lives. What happens when regardless of the title, you aren't fulfilled in the work you're doing? Despite the hard work, long hours of development, and a great network, you're unfulfilled and feel called to more.

You've read those stories, right? The stories of brilliant people in high-powered and high-pressure roles with big titles and six-figure salaries who are unhappy in their careers. This sense of being unfulfilled can quickly turn from just disliking your job to also disliking yourself. So much of our professional experiences blend in with our personal experiences and vice versa. An article in the Harvard Business Review called "What Happens When Your Career Becomes Your Whole Identity" shares that psychologists refer to this as enmeshment—when the boundaries between people and individual identities become blurred or lose importance. "Enmeshment prevents the development of a stable, independent sense of self."[4]

Our career, income, and social status can influence other people's perception of our identity. The Journal of Social Psychology published an article in 2007 by Elizabeth Aries and Maynard Seider entitled, "The Role of Social Class in the Formation of Identity" that states how students from both public and elite private colleges" ranked occupational goals as first in importance to identity and social class as

---

[4] Janna Koretz, "What Happens When Your Career Becomes Your Whole Identity," Harvard Business Review, Accessed May 9, 2020. https://hbr.org/2019/12/what-happens-when-your-career-becomes-your-whole-identity

second. The affluent students regarded social class as significantly more important to identity than did the lower-income students."[5]

> *Our career, income, and social status can influence other people's perception of our identity.*

Beyond this study of students, I've experienced this play out in boardrooms and meetings throughout my career. How often do we equate the worth and identity of others with how senior their title is? This can be especially challenging when we're at a crossroads in our career, and our roles change. I've managed these transitions by keeping this quote from Chase Consumer Bank CEO, Thasunda Duckett, top of mind, "I rent my title, but I own my character." Our titles are temporary, even the big ones. If we believe this, then we must also believe that our career isn't the core of our identity.

There can be so many mental and emotional challenges that come with our careers. Besides working in a high-pressure environment, the emotional tax many of us with intersectional identities experience adds a deeper layer of complexity to how we view ourselves and the decisions we make regarding our career. How would you introduce yourself if you couldn't share what you do?

---

[5] Elizabeth Aries and Maynard Seider, "The Role of Social Class in the Formation of Identity: A Study of Public and Elite Private College Students," The Journal of Social Psychology. May 2007. Pg. 151

CAREER AND IDENTITY AS A BLACK WOMAN

Black women are underrepresented in leadership roles in the workplace and often underestimated, overlooked, and underpaid. As Black women, we don't have the luxury of mediocrity. Due to the career promotion, salary, business investment, and capital inequities that exist for women that look like me, there's often an added pressure to perform and prove by any means necessary. If we aren't mindful, our worth can very quickly become synonymous with what we achieve professionally. As such, this can cause us to ground who we are in the title we've worked harder to earn, the salary it took longer to amass, and the company it took blood, sweat, tears, and extra years to build.

All of this can lead to emotional and mental challenges; we don't feel we can acknowledge or address. If we are honest with ourselves, many of us are grieving. No one has died physically, but perhaps we've lost a sense of our routine, a project opportunity, a relationship, a job, or even our sense of well-being, satisfaction, and confidence. What does grief look like in the workplace? I'm glad you asked!

CAREER GRIEF

As we discussed, grief is a natural emotion of complex, conflicting, and frequently unpredictable feelings in response to a loss or change that disrupts a familiar pattern or prevents the desired outcome. Although we don't typically associate career changes and transitions with grief, there are many ways grief can manifest at work. Here are some of the ways we can experience career grief:

> *Although we don't typically associate career changes and transitions with grief, there are many ways grief can manifest at work.*

1. MANAGING MICRO-AGGRESSIONS AND TOXIC TEAMMATES

The first nine years of my corporate career I spent in sales. From day one, I was the overachiever, high-performing leader— even before the promoted titles. I spent time learning from people who were in senior roles within and beyond my team. I observed their communication style, how they interacted in meetings, the projects they were working on, and even shadowed them to learn more about the exact behaviors that helped them succeed.

After three years in, I applied for a promotion. I didn't get it the first time, but I received some valuable feedback and turned that hiring manager into an advocate for the next role I went after. For every feedback area, I took action and initiated a time to follow up to share what I was learning along the way. I needed more leadership stories? Got that experience. Required to show proficiency with project management? Got those experiences. Needed more examples of leading a strategic plan? Got those experiences. Needed to win President's Club? Won that too! My partner and I were the number one and number two sales representatives in the country that year. Every hurdle, I jumped over it with the support of some awesome teammates and mentors. When it came time for the next opportunity, I was the obvious choice. I got the senior sales role and relocated from Nashville to Chattanooga.

Little did I know this relocation would be met with micro-aggressions and a toxic teammate who would teach me how to lead difficult people. During my first few weeks, I scheduled 1:1 lunch or breakfast meetings to get to know my new teammates. Everyone I reached out to was very responsive and excited about meeting to connect and learn more about each other. However, it took about three calls to connect with one of my teammates, and she was less than enthusiastic about my lunch invitation. I'll never forget how she showed up twenty minutes late with another teammate (I guess as back up) and shared with me that she didn't understand how I got the job over her. That lunch meeting didn't go as planned! About two weeks into the role, my hiring manager was promoted to a new position. Despite her resistance and rudeness early on, I decided to view my relationship with her as another hurdle I would clear in due time.

Over time, it became clear that she wasn't just rude, short, and challenging to work with towards me, but she was this way with others on the team as well. The manager who hired me knew how she was. But with our new manager, I knew I had to go even higher every time she went low because he was still getting to know both of us.

One day our new manager asked me to share a conference experience with the rest of the team on our monthly team call. I was one of two colleagues who had attended this event where most of my team did not. We were asked to share learnings and valuable takeaways with the team. Of course, I was happy to share and created a couple of slides with clear examples of ways to apply the new insight into our business to improve our sales as a team. My teammates asked questions throughout my overview. Our manager thanked me for sharing. Several colleagues sent follow-up emails and texts sharing how they appreciated me making the insights relevant to their business's nuances.

A week later, my manager called to share "some feedback from the team" about our call. He shared how he'd received some feedback about my approach on the call, and it came across as if I was "telling the team what to do." I was shocked and also grateful we are on the phone and not in person. I picked my jaw up off the floor and asked for him to help me understand the feedback, share his perspective on my delivery of the implementation approach, and what I could do differently next time. I was taken aback by the entire conversation, yet I still wanted to know how I could improve. I've never heard so much backtracking and side-stepping in all my days. The feedback was vague, and he eventually shared that he disagreed with the feedback but wanted to make sure he shared it.

I felt frustrated and sad when I got off that call. My manager, of all people, knew how hard I was working, yet I was fluctuating between "Was I coming off in a bossy way? That wasn't my intention." And "I already know who said it, and her bias isn't unconscious." Not to mention, "Why would he even call me with this crap!"

After thinking through all the angles and since this was the feedback received and I was in a leadership role, I decided to call everyone on my team to check-in, share the feedback, apologize if they were offended, and get their thoughts on my delivery. As you can imagine, all my teammates except one were shocked by the feedback I'd received. They complimented my presentation, and several even apologized to me that I had to deal with this. It was clear who shared the feedback. It also was apparent I was being tested and taught how to deal with beyond difficult people. I decided that because I was experiencing it, there was an opportunity to learn from it.

Have you had a toxic teammate like this before? I share this story because although this was far from the only bad experience with her, much of the stress I endured resulted from moments like this—microaggressions, racial inequities, and a lack of leadership to address what was happening. From her calling my manager to share feedback about me to discrediting my earned recognition and leadership, I was stressed! This is the emotional workplace trauma that can often show up as grief. It can look like trying to navigate experiences of a loss of trust, loss of confidence, or loss of influence. This grief can cause us to doubt our capabilities, capacity, and confidence in our positions and the ones we're striving for next.

> *This grief can cause us to doubt our capabilities, capacity, and confidence in our positions and the ones we're striving for next.*

I thought I was taking the high road and choosing when (seldom) to directly respond to the toxic behavior for fear of being labeled the angry, problematic (and only) black woman. When, in most cases, I was likely contributing to the build-up of my trauma and grief because I chose not to speak up. There are many moments I can recall now where I wish the younger me would've advocated for myself and addressed the toxicity that I was experiencing openly and directly.

When I consider Black people's historical trauma in America and how we've centered whiteness as a way to survive in the workplace, I believe now more than ever it's important to address microaggressions and bias directly.

Here are some ways you can respond to initiate conversations when you are experiencing a microaggression:

- **PICK YOUR BATTLE** — Every microaggression may not necessarily need to be called out or addressed the same way. Depending on the context, what is said, and who is saying it be wise in your response. Sometimes it's better to lose the battle and win the war. Also, keep in mind the place, timing, and approach if you do decide to respond.

- **SEEK TO UNDERSTAND BEFORE TRYING TO BE UNDERSTOOD** — This is Habit #5 in Steven Covey's best-selling book The 7 Habits of Highly Successful People. "What makes you think that? Can you help me understand why you have that opinion?" If you lead with the priority of understanding the other person's point of view, it will 1. Give you time to think past your emotions. 2. Allow you to respond in a more informed way to ensure you're addressing the core issue— the behavior, not the person.

- **THE BOOKEND CONVERSATION** — Start positive with an appreciation for the time to connect, have the crucial conversation, and end on an aligned note. More than ended positive, you want to close the conversation with mutual understanding and hopefully a better connection. Ensure your colleague knows your intention to bring awareness to how their comment made you feel and how it could be perceived. Then thank them for allowing both of you to have the conversation.

- **USE "I" STATEMENTS AFTER YOU'VE ASKED CLARIFYING QUESTIONS** — Begin the conversation with inquiry to allow the person to describe what he or she meant before sharing your I statements. This is important to prioritize empathy in the conversation. I statements (instead of you statements) help address the behavior, not the person. For example, you may say, "I felt hurt when you said ..." This helps ensure the conversation is centered on the behavior and not the person. We all have biases, and becoming more aware of it is excellent, but what we can change and measure is behavior.

- **HAVE THE CONVERSATION IN PERSON, OR ON A VIDEO CALL AT THE VERY LEAST** — I'd think this is a no-brainer, but try to refrain from addressing a microaggression via text or email. Face-to-face allows you to match your non-verbal communication with your message and assess your colleague's non-verbal communication. Your non-verbal communication will be more important than the words you choose to use as it makes up 93% of communication.

No one is immune from bias. Anyone can find themselves on the opposite end of a microaggression making an unintentional hurtful comment to someone. I believe this is the responsibility of each of us—regardless of demographic—to speak up, reach out, and build inclusive work environments because these are ways grief can manifest at work.

Even in the most toxic environments, you always learn something. Every experience is an opportunity for continuous improvement! Although I had several unpleasant experiences with this teammate, I learned how to make challenging moments at work, work for me. I developed the skill of working with difficult people. As a result, I was able to turn this woeful relationship into a successful partnership and even mentorship. I knew or relationship had shifted when she asked me to review her resume, share advice on her STAR interview stories, and help her pursue promotion opportunities.

> *Even in the most toxic environments, you always learn something. Every experience is an opportunity for continuous improvement.*

2. LEAVING THE JOB AND LAYOFFS

Another common way grief manifests at work is when we apply for a promotion or new opportunity, prepare for the process and don't get the job. Or when we've worked hard and invested so much time at a company, and then we end up on the layoff list. The redirection almost always feels like rejection when these things happen. Yes, we know rejection is often redirection; and what's for us won't pass us. We also know that all things will work together for our good. At the same time, we have genuine feelings of frustration, disappointment, and loss when unplanned professional shifts happen. None of us likes rejection, even when it comes with excellent feedback after not getting the job. The job search process for a new opportunity can send us spiraling into feelings of despair, frustration, exhaustion, self-doubt, and even anger. Has interviewing ever caused you to feel this way?

In the 1969 book On Death and Dying by Elisabeth Kübler-Ross, she introduces the Five Stages of Grief, often referred to as the DABDA model. As we've discussed, we need to be aware that these feelings of grief aren't only isolated to the loss of a loved one. We can experience these phases with any loss, including those that impact our careers. According to the EKR Foundation, a non-profit organization inspired by the life of psychiatrist, humanitarian, and hospice pioneer, Dr. Elisabeth Kübler-Ross, here are the Five Stages of Grief [6]:

- **DENIAL** – Shock or rejection is usually the first stage in the Kubler-Ross Model. In this phase, we put on a temporary defense mechanism and process this new disturbing reality. We can fluctuate between the shock of is this happening to denial that it did.

- **ANGER** – When the realization finally hits, and we understand the gravity of the situation, we may become angry and look for someone to blame. Anger can be manifested or expressed in many ways. Some may take it out on themselves. Others may direct it towards people around them. You may find yourself irritable, frustrated, and short-tempered during this stage.

- **BARGAINING** – When the stage of anger passes away, we may start thinking about ways to postpone the inevitable and try to find out the best thing left in the situation. This can include trying to negotiate in the situation and come to the point of compromise. Bargaining may help develop a sustainable solution and bring relief to those who are moving close to what they wish to avoid altogether.

- **DEPRESSION** – Depression is a stage in which we may feel sadness, fear, regret, guilt, and other negative emotions. We may

---

[6] Dr. Elisabeth Kübler-Ross, "Kübler-Ross Change Curve®." Elisabeth Kübler-Ross Foundation, EKR Family, 1969. https://www.ekrfoundation.org/5-stages-of-grief/change-curve/

have completely given up by now and may now reach a dead-end from where the road only seems dark. You may notice signs of indifference, reclusiveness, pushing others away, and zero excitement towards most things in life. Some common symptoms of depression include sadness, low energy, feeling demotivated, losing trust in God, etc.

- **ACCEPTANCE** – Once we realize that fighting the change that has come into our life will not make the grief go away, we lean into accepting it completely. The accepting attitude may not be a comfortable space initially but is one in which we may stop resisting change and move ahead with it.

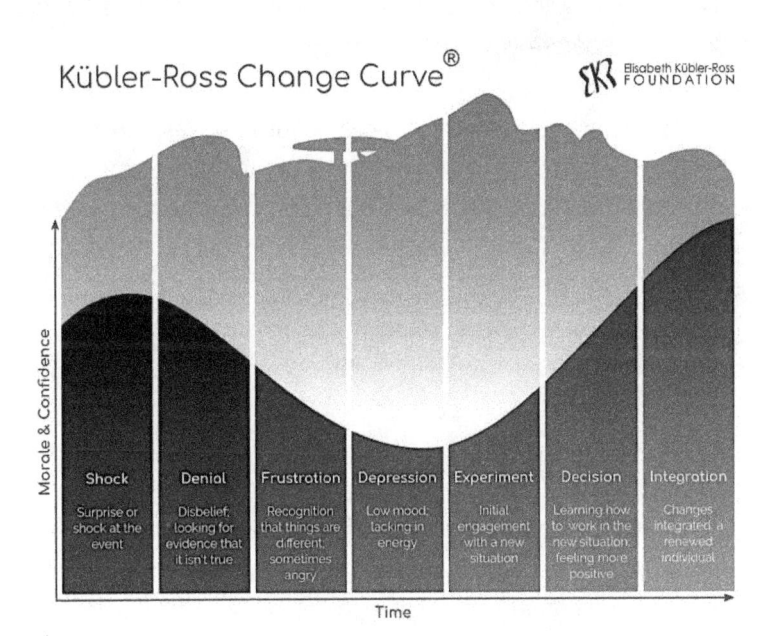

Kübler-Ross Change Curve®

Elisabeth Kübler-Ross FOUNDATION

Morale & Confidence vs. Time

Shock	Surprise or shock at the event
Denial	Disbelief; looking for evidence that it isn't true
Frustration	Recognition that things are different; sometimes angry
Depression	Low mood; lacking in energy
Experiment	Initial engagement with a new situation
Decision	Learning how to work in the new situation; feeling more positive
Integration	Changes integrated; a renewed individual

We often experience these same stages when it comes to the loss of a job opportunity. For many of us, our career becomes a symbolic representation of our identity, and disruption in what we do can cause us to question who we are. Here is an example of how these Five Stages of Grief can look with job loss:

- **DENIAL** – You start hearing the layoff rumors. The company is going through a restructuring, and you know people will be impacted. You refuse to think it will happen to you, though. How could it? You're a top performer, and you represent the diversity your organization needs to elevate. You get the call that your role will be eliminated, and you're in a layoff wave. You immediately think there must be some misunderstanding. There isn't. You've been given a 60-day notice period before your last day of work.

- **ANGER** – As you start to learn more about who was and who wasn't impacted, you become frustrated. "How are they safe, and I'm not?" You begin to question why this is happening despite the value you bring to the team. Certainly, someone should've said you don't belong on the layoff list.

- **BARGAINING** – You start to think through the possibilities. You talk to your manager about opportunities to post for roles in other departments. You don't see any opportunities that excite you, but shouldn't you just pick a position in any function to stay on the bus? Anything is better than being laid off, right? You reach out to several mentors, your coach and talk things over with your family. Your colleagues are sharing potential, upcoming openings that could work for you.

- **DEPRESSION** – As you get closer to your last day of work, you start to feel the heaviness and sadness of what's happening. You've worked hard for twelve years and feel deflated that you've still ended up here. You want to be somewhere where you're celebrated and not tolerated. At the same time, you think it will be tough to find another role like the one you are in. You feel like giving up. You become less interested in looking for opportunities within your organization and are more reserved in your communication with everyone.

- **ACCEPTANCE** – You start to come to terms with the reality of leaving the organization and feel confident in your decision despite not having all the answers. You affirm, "I'm making the best decision for me. This chapter is closing, and a new one is beginning. Everything will be alright, and I will thrive through this." You embrace your reality and confidently share your decision to accept the severance and leave the company.

This wasn't a scenario I had to hypothesize about. In 2019, this was essentially my journey through these stages of grief. I was faced with an unexpected layoff and decided to accept the outcome and use the redirection as an opportunity to leap into entrepreneurship full time. Does this resonate? Eventually, we will cycle through these stages as we are faced with grief. It's important to note we must give ourselves grace through these moments. It's your journey, at your pace, where you can decide the next best move for you.

3. NOT GETTING THE JOB

What do you do when you're interviewing and don't get the job? How do you respond when you've spent countless hours preparing for an opportunity, sharing with people you admire and respect, asking mentors and sponsors to support you in the interview process with a recommendation? Then you don't get the job. Often when this happens, there can be a tendency to shy away from posting for similar opportunities again. Or you may get discouraged and decide to just focus on where we are. There can even be feelings of embarrassment and shame associated with not having an ideal outcome in a job search process, mostly when you're repeatedly rejected. The easy thing to do in those moments is to hide or to say, "I'm just going to lay low and let this pass over." However, I would encourage you to do the opposite. Continue to show up for yourself. You are your biggest advocate, and moments like this are when your character is shown. It's where you cement your personal brand. It's where you reinvent yourself. It's where you become relentless in your pursuit, and against all odds, you achieve your desired outcome! I don't share this because it sounds good. I believe this to be true because that's exactly what happened to me. Remember when I shared with you I realized I was grieving even though no one had died while in small group Bible study? Here's is the story on how that happened.

THE VIAGRA STORY

Yes, I have a story about Viagra—indirectly speaking. I was about six years into my pharmaceutical sales career when I decided to apply for a marketing position for the first time. It had been a solid three years since I'd added this aspiration to my individual development plan, and I was working the plan to gain this experience. When this role came up, not only was I excited about the opportunity, I also was thrilled this role was reporting to one of the best marketing leaders at our organization. Her reputation proceeded her as a brilliant marketer and one of a few people leaders in the space who was also an excellent developer of people. The icing on the cake was this would all happen working on an iconic brand.

Despite being told it was improbable to transition from sales to marketing on the first try (sidenote: their experience may look nothing like your experience), I was the number one candidate and was offered the job! I can still remember to this day my failed attempt to suppress a scream when the hiring manager called with the news late on a Friday evening so I wouldn't be held in suspense over the weekend. I was pumped! We were seven weeks out from getting married, and one of my first calls was to my wedding planner to add an NYC theme to our décor! New York, here I come... or so I thought.

Enter disruption. Of course, it's only after the offer is made that you get all the details on the package, the timeline for moving, etc. Although this was a fantastic role in my dream city and on an excellent team, there were some unforeseen challenges. From the compensation package and lack of relocation support to learning that my soon-to-be husband would receive a full scholarship to get his MBA at Emory Goizueta Business School, it turned out that this immediate move to NYC wouldn't work for us in 2014. Therefore, I had to make one of the most challenging professional decisions in my career and turn down the offer. Although I knew this was best for my family, I was devastated. Not only that but once I made this decision, all hell broke loose, and I began (what I didn't realize then) to grieve this missed opportunity and loss of trust amongst colleagues.

As soon as the news hit that I'd turned down this big job, the stories started swirling and took on a life of their own. It was one of the hardest seasons of my career. Beyond having to re-align with sponsors, supporters, and stakeholders who had rallied and sent recommendations on my behalf to get the role, there were 3-4 times the people who thought they were also privy to an explanation. At this point, I had three choices—leave and take a sales or marketing role at another organization, put my head down and wait until the storm passed over, or pick my head up and show up anyway.

SHOW UP ANYWAY

Yes, you guessed it! We show up and thrive through it around here! However, please believe I didn't feel as confident then as I am sharing with you now. My imposter syndrome was at an all time high during this time. I remember having to affirm myself before and during meetings to not only show up but speak up despite the whispers. It got to a point where I had to decide if I would be laid back and let everyone else tell my story with the variable endings or choose to own my narrative and rebuild my personal brand. The last straw in making this decision was at a national sales meeting. There were nearly one thousand sales colleagues present as well as all of our marketing teams. I remember the moment I decided it was time for me to show up, speak up, and own my narrative when I overheard a marketer telling her teammate, "Yeah, that's her. The one who turned down the role." From that moment on, I decided, you know what, this happened. It's unfortunate, but I'm not going to shrink and be ostracized for my decision. If anyone wants to talk to me, I'm willing to talk about it. But I will not allow these awkward moments and people with half of the story making false claims to cause me to have my head down and not show up the way I know I can.

One of the ways we show up is by being exceptional at following up. If you applied for a role and didn't get it or have had a similar experience where you walked away from an opportunity, follow up with that hiring manager. Connect with the colleagues you interviewed to thank them for the opportunity, request feedback, and determine your connection cadence for building those relationships. Get feedback on your interview skills, gaps in your experiences, ways you can improve to be a stronger candidate for similar opportunities, etc. Before ending the call, you could follow up with, "Before we wrap up, I would love to schedule some time to check-in and update you on how I am tracking the feedback you shared. When would be a good day for you next 8–10 weeks? I appreciate it." These are some ways you can make sure you're showing up and engaging in valuable feedback conversations with your interviewers.

> *One of the ways we show up is by being exceptional at following up.*

Another way to show up when you don't get the job you want is by having those courageous conversations. And I believe it's so essential to have courageous conversations because they help you identify the depth of your loss. It was critical to be strategic in going back and connecting with people when you don't get the job opportunity, promotion, or project. When you take ownership of your experience in this way, it shows your character and priority of accomplishing the goal you set out to achieve. Whether the courageous conversation is to request more specific feedback or to clarify a decision you've made that others don't agree with, remember you are your biggest advocate, so show up for yourself and own your narrative.

Initiating these courageous conversations was exactly what I had to do with the Viagra story. However, before I got to that point, I had to ask myself some tough questions to clarify where I was before communicating with someone else. I had to do some introspection to uncover, "What else did I lose when I didn't accept the job?" What is it that you lose when you go for a job and don't get it? Aside from the job experience or other obvious external shifts, what else lies beneath the surface?

WHAT EXACTLY DID YOU LOSE?

When it was all said and done, what I had lost was the confidence and trust of the people who supported me. Beyond the specific opportunity to move into this new position at this time, I lost the advantage of learning how to be a marketer with this particular team and this hiring manager. My reputation also took a hit—from being a go-getter and high achiever to being indecisive and unwilling to sacrifice for a great opportunity. Those were the things beneath the surface of the Viagra loss. What made it hard wasn't just the missed career opportunity.

I knew another role would come around again, and I believed I would have another shot. The damage to my reputation and audacity of so many colleagues that shared misinformation was also connected to this experience.

As I got clear about what I lost, I also began to see what I'd gained. One of the beautiful things about adversity is that it shows you, you, and it shows you who's genuinely for you. If this experience didn't happen, I would've continued to invest in disingenuous relationships. Through this experience, I gained depth with some significant relationships and a loyal circle of supporters who lifted me up when I needed it most and are still mentors and close friends who I'm so grateful for to this day.

Everyone loves you when you're winning. But when you take a hit, it reveals who's down for the recognition and with whom you have substantive and trusted relationships. "Oh, I support you. You let me know what I can do to help out," looks much different when you're the center of adversity. I gained so much wisdom and insight into workplace politics through this experience. Some of the same people who supported me in going after the Viagra opportunity were the same ones in calibration meetings speaking negatively about me. While you're looking at your loss, be sure to take note of the lessons you've gained. This experience taught me who I could trust, and it showed me what I wanted more clearly than I'd known before. This wouldn't have happened

> *While you're looking at your loss, be sure to take note of the lessons you've gained.*

without the loss, introspection, and the courageous conversations, so I could identify, "What exactly did I lose?"

FAILING FORWARD WITH FORTITUDE

Once I was clear on my gains and losses, it was time to focus forward. We often talk about failing forward in the context of businesses and innovation. Yet, sometimes we can maximize the failure and minimize the importance of moving forward when it comes to our personal/professional failures. When I experienced this failure and loss of relationships, brand equity, and trust, I had to sit down and think through a strategy for building a new bridge to where I knew I wanted to be. I remember sitting down with a journal and making a list of everyone I needed to speak with to "reinforce the bridge." I knew that rebuilding by brand would require intention and grit, and the focus had to be on how to move forward.

One of the first people on my list was the Viagra hiring manager. I had to go back to her to ensure she was clear on why I made the decision I did and determine how to continue building our relationship. It was so awkward at first! I got the cold shoulder the first couple of times I reached out. But little by little, she realized my persistence was authentic, and my aspiration to be a marketer was still just as genuine as when I'd interviewed with her. Whenever I'd have an opportunity to go to New York for an interview for another brand, or for a project, I made sure she knew about it and asked for time to connect while there. Over time, she became one of my biggest sponsors, who helped me land what I like to call my red-carpet marketing role in 2017.

> *How are you staying committed to your aspirations in the face of challenges and rejection?*

How are you staying committed to your aspirations in the face of challenges and rejection? Are you continuing to show up? If this career opportunity or this project is what you truly want, you won't give up on it. I applied for nine different positions between the Viagra role and the marketing role I accepted. The marketing role I landed and accepted was my tenth try after the Viagra role, and it was tailor-made for me with a full relocation package! There were plenty of people telling me I needed to shift my career development down a different path, but I knew I wanted to be a marketer at my organization. I'm so grateful for the great circle of support I had to help me reach that goal after a very public career loss! Are you maintaining your authenticity, even as you're thriving through adversity?

You only get a chance to rebound after a missed shot. Sometimes we have this perspective that when things don't happen the way we want them to—when we don't get the job or don't get the project or promotion or were laid off—then it means something is wrong with us or that we are going down the wrong path. That does not have to be your story. Some of the greatest athletes and some of the greatest moments in sports history and even businesses are cultivated after a missed shot. Why? Primarily because of how you position yourself for the rebound, to shoot it back up, and try again! If you're in a season where you're shooting and missing career opportunities, I want to encourage you to keep shooting by positioning yourself to rebound!

Here are three tips to position yourself for a rebound and slam dunk during the job search process:

- First, your response to not getting the job is critical. Express gratitude for the opportunity and then ask for feedback. If you've interviewed with multiple people, ask to schedule a time for a feedback discussion with the other interviewers. Not only will this give you insight into ways to continuously improve, but it will also help you build new relationships.

- Next, give yourself time to process. Hold space for how you're feeling as a result of the news. Invest some time in introspection reviewing your interview responses, job search strategy, etc. In what ways can you tighten things up? Were there insights you gained on the response/feedback call you need to note for next time? What actionable feedback did you receive?

- Lastly, make the adjustments and continue to be your best advocate. Whether the feedback is actionable or not, consider what adjustments will be in your best interest. Do you need to tweak your response to a commonly asked question? Do you need to polish up your interview set up and answer to the "tell me about yourself" question? Do you need to follow up with someone you met during the process who could connect you to other opportunities? Assess your next best move, then make a plan to follow up and continue advocating for yourself.

4. PROMOTIONS AND GROWING PAINS

The last example I'll share on how grief can manifest at work is through positive change. We may not typically associate positive situations with grief, but the transition from one dimension to the next level includes losing what's been familiar. Consider a time when perhaps you've had to relocate. Although you may have been excited about the move and the opportunity to experience and explore a new place, you also likely processed what it would mean to leave what you had become accustomed to in your current location. The loss of your usual routine, spending time with your circle in that space, and even the routine of the places you enjoyed going to are all replaced with newness when moving from one home to the next. The same can be true for promotion or growth experiences that don't involve relocation—we experience a change that includes losing what we've grown accustomed to. Although these changes are often where growth happens, it's essential to be aware of how they may impact our mental and emotional wellbeing.

What other workplace experiences would you add to this list that can trigger a grief response?

_____
_____
_____
_____
_____
_____

Thoughts along the journey:

2. Identify the Loss

Let's think about where you are in your career right now. If you are currently (or recently) in the midst of a change, transition, or challenge, list what you actually lost.

1. What has been your most recent career change?

2. What has made it difficult? List three ways this change has impacted you.

3. What did you have before that you no longer have access to now?

4. How has losing this impacted you?

5. What adjustments have you made?

6. Where do you want to be?

7. What conversations have you had?

SECTION TWO

GRIT

"Some people mistake grit for sheer persistence – charging up the same hill again and again. But that's not quite what I mean by the word 'grit.' You want to minimize friction and find the most effective, most efficient way forward. You might actually have more grit if you treat your energy as a precious commodity."

– REID HOFFMAN
CO-FOUNDER AND EXECUTIVE CHAIRMAIN OF LINKEDIN

CHAPTER 3
Survival Mode Isn't Sustainable
I couldn't heal because I tried to hide the hurt

What have you been taught about grief? Think about it. Out of all the lessons you've been instructed, has anyone ever shared with you about grief when you weren't journeying through it? I ask this question because, well, I was never taught about grief—only grit. Experience would be my first teacher with grief. I'm much more familiar with grit. My mother—one of the first Black students to integrate the University of South Carolina and an award-winning sales professional turned social worker—was my first teacher on grit. Her lessons prepared me for my corporate career.

WHAT IS GRIT?

Grit is defined as the firmness of mind and spirit or unyielding courage in the face of hardship or danger. People with grit are often recognized as being fearless, confident, and resilient. My parents taught me this quality when I'd be met with a challenge as the only girl on an all-boys basketball league or come home dejected after being teased for being the tallest fifth-grader on the bus in middle school. My parents would affirm who I was, whose I was, and help me understand that what I was undergoing didn't define me. I appreciate those lessons.

As women, many of our encounters with change, transition, and loss often lead us to a similar response to power through. As Black women specifically, we're conditioned to embody what it means to be courageous and walk through life with fortitude in every area of life. We learn lessons such as, "You have to be twice as good to get half as much" early in our life and career. As such, we often journey through life with our cape and mask, in survival mode, to prove we belong in spaces often systemically designed without our consideration; and, dare I say, designed to keep us contained. I've observed these nuances in Black women's lives from my mother to colleagues in corporate America, and even as I reflect on my own life. If we aren't mindful, we can find ourselves operating from a steady state of survival mode. We will come back to the impact of our cultural identity on this topic in a moment. But first, what exactly is survival mode?

> *As Black women specifically, we're conditioned to embody what it means to be courageous and walk through life with fortitude in every area of life.*

If we aren't mindful, we can find ourselves operating from a steady state of survival mode.

HAS SURVIVAL MODE BECOME YOUR WAY OF LIVING?

Physiologically, our nervous system is one of the most intricate and powerful structures in our body. Its function is to receive information on our environment and determine the appropriate response. You've likely heard of the two ways our nervous system functions: sensory functions (our five primary senses that receive information) and motor functions (our voluntary and involuntary response to that info). It's our nervous system that senses, interprets, and responds to our understanding of safety in any environment. When our body senses we aren't safe, our nervous system shifts to "survival mode" to protect us from what appears to be an unsafe environment. In these moments, we fight, flight, or freeze. Sound familiar?

You've experienced this in many moments. Think back to a time you walked into a networking event with people you didn't know well, perhaps people who were different from you. If you're an introvert, you may find these networking events make you anxious, hyper-aware of how long they will last, and looking for any and every opportunity to exit the room to gather yourself. As an introvert, I have experienced this flight feeling before in settings such as this.

Or perhaps you've experienced a microaggression in the workplace— that unexpected and debatably unintentional comment from a colleague that leaves you vacillating between reacting how you want to and responding how you opt to. In moments like this, I've fluctuated between "I know she didn't just say that to me!" (fight) and

"Did she just say what I think she said? Does she know what that means? Should I say something? I don't want to come off as the angry Black woman." (freeze)

These experiences and many others can trigger a survival mode response of:

- **FIGHT** – Anger, Argument, Insult
- **FLIGHT** – Avoidance, Denial, Sabotage
- **FREEZE** – Shut Down, Justify, Stall

These are examples of fight, flight, or freeze responses resulting from natural, hormonal physiological reactions triggered by a psychological fear. Our switch to survival mode in our body is a fear-based reaction that first starts in our mind. Typically, what we fear is conditioned by our direct or vicarious experiences. Whenever we encounter this perceived threat, our brain thinks we're in danger, and our body automatically reacts to a fight, flight, or freeze response to keep us safe. If we aren't mindful, these can become our default responses, especially in work environments where we don't believe we belong. What experiences have you had that triggered a survival mode response?

> *Our switch to survival mode in our body is a fear-based reaction that first starts in our mind.*

SURVIVING VS. THRIVING IN THE WORKPLACE

After turning down the Viagra role at the end of 2014 and spending two years owning my narrative, owning my development, and going after the marketing experience I'd always wanted; I finally landed a role tailor-made for me in February 2017! Now, let's talk about what happened after I said yes. We had relocated to NYC from Chattanooga, and I was so thrilled to be in my new marketing role. I had transitioned from my flexible field sales days to our corporate headquarters holding this dream job in Midtown Manhattan and getting to know my new manager. Although I couldn't quite put my finger on what made our first few meetings more awkward than expected, I was excited to work with him because his entire career was brand management, so I knew I would learn so much just by being in the room with him. I was anxious to understand the role and skills of a marketer and how to think like one as well.

As I got more acquainted with the HQ marketing culture, it became clear early that many of the people leaders were in those roles due to marketing expertise rather than people leadership capability. Despite noticing these gaps, I was committed to showing up and doing everything within my power to support my leader and exceed expectations. Our first few weeks working together went something like this. He would ask me to do something with minimal directions. I would clarify to ensure I was aligned with his expectations and would leverage my team for insights to complete the task. Once I'd circle back with him, he would share how most of the work I'd done was wrong or not how he would approach it. I remember thinking surely there's a better way to communicate than where we were.

At the same time, almost as soon as I moved to NYC my mother got sick and was in and out of the hospital. I was on a plane every other Friday to spend the weekend with her. Because things were so rocky with my manager, I didn't feel comfortable sharing about the simultaneous family challenges. I was concerned with showing up well and proving I belonged there to hopefully iron out the kinks with my new leader. On some visits back to Nashville, my mom was in the hospital. During others, she was doing better, and I would spend the weekend with her at home. As a family, we were preparing and prayerful that she would continue to gain her strength to have major heart surgery in the summer of 2017. For most of my first two months in the position, I was back and forth, navigating a new role, learning a new way of living, and trying to make a connection with a new leader who was in and out of the country. I was fluctuating in and out of (mostly in) survival mode.

At the time, I didn't realize I was surviving that first couple of months as a way of living. I would be one of the first members of the team in the office in the morning and one of the last to leave in the evening to navigate the self-guided onboarding, learn my new team and meet all of my new agency and cross-functional partners. On days I would leave right at or just after 5pm, I'd rush out to meet a broker to view apartments before dark. Within those first few weeks, I was also assigned to lead an innovative, national project with visibility across the entire commercial organization. I was being stretched in every way, but I knew I could handle it. After all, this was a new role in a new function, and I just had to get over this initial learning curve. In the meantime, we also were looking at new apartments to move from our terrible first Upper East Side apartment.

Approximately six weeks into navigating this turbulence, I had a catch-up call with one of my mentors and sponsors—we'll call him Caleb. This call turned my intermittent survival mode into overdrive. Caleb was a sales leader in Nashville but was close with my new manager (let's call him Ryan). Up until this point, I hadn't leveraged his insight to ask about my experiences with Ryan. I thought it was vital for me to develop a relationship with Ryan based on my experiences without the bias filter of what everyone else thought of him. I'd scheduled a routine call with Caleb to check-in, share my new big project and what I was learning so far, and gain additional insight into best practices for working with my new agency partners. This agenda halted when Caleb began our meeting telling me he was so glad I reached out because he was going to reach out to me. He said Ryan reached out to him to get some advice on some concerns he had about me, and he wanted to share the conversation with me. Now, as you can probably imagine, my fight, flight, and freeze modes were all activated.

Immediately my heartbeat sped up. My mind raced to try to recall what possible concerns Ryan could've had during the past six weeks, three of which he was out of the country, where he hadn't had the opportunity to address them with me? After all, I had become a contortionist at asking for specific feedback. Caleb went on to share that Ryan was concerned about when I was leaving the office and how I was implementing his feedback on my work. I was shocked.

As I opened my mouth to formulate a response, I thanked Caleb for letting me know and shared how Ryan never said anything to me about any issues, problems, questions, or concerns. Aside from instructions on my first project, all of his feedback had been positive, "You're on the right track. You're doing well. Great job, etc." However, that wasn't what he was sharing in the rooms I wasn't in, and that's the story that counts.

From this conversation, I concluded that any discussion about my mother's health and my desire to discuss a work from Nashville plan to spend more time with her would have to wait. I rationalized this survival mode response by focusing on going even farther above and beyond to prove I belonged on this team and was more than capable of exceeding expectations. I felt every emotion you're probably thinking, from anger to sadness, and proceeded with my guard up, triple checking that my I's were dotted and T's crossed, and conversations were documented to protect myself at all costs. I wanted my leader to value my contribution, communicate honestly to build trust, and know that I was more than capable of being an exceptional marketer. Thus, I proceeded with my insane work and travel schedule, balancing the office's calls with my mother's cardiologist and my dad for another six weeks, until June 5, 2017.

SURVIVAL MODE ISN'T SUSTAINABLE

It was Monday, June 5, 2017, and I was ready for a productive week. I had a big meeting that morning, and I was pumped! Have you ever had that feeling? You have a big presentation, and you feel prepared, confident, and convinced this moment will shift your career experiences? This is precisely how I felt! I was meeting with my manager's manager, and I had a great rapport with her. I also knew this presentation would be another proof point to Ryan that I was an asset to his team. I was ready to hit a homerun and even wore my special suit jacket I had custom made in Thailand for an extra boost of confidence!

It was roughly forty-five minutes before my meeting when I stepped into the elevator from the fourth floor to head down to the lobby for a cup of coffee. I walked out of the elevator and waved at one of my favorite colleagues on the security team. She always greeted me with a huge smile in the mornings and complimented my red lipstick. If she was working at the door, I knew I'd be coming or leaving with a smile. As I walked towards the coffee shop, I noticed my phone notification light blinking. It was my dad calling. As I answered the phone, I heard something I'd never heard before. He was crying. In a loud, shrieking voice full of tears and anguish, he repeated for the third time what I heard him say twice before but didn't want to believe. "She's braindead!" My knees buckled under me as I collapsed onto the floor, trying to grasp what he said. The security team rushed over to check on me and help me to my feet. Somehow, I made it back to the fourth floor. A leader on our team scheduled a flight for me. I called my husband, hopped in a taxi, and met him to head to the airport.

My world was caving in as I tried to process all of the possibilities through my tears and pain. In my mind, I envisioned myself leaving my organization and becoming a full-time caregiver to my mother. I'd watched her do the same thing with my grandmother. My grandmother had Alzheimer's and lived with us. My brothers and I helped my parents take care of her for years. It would've been my honor to take care of my mom for as long as the Lord allowed. Through prayers and puffy eyes, I envisioned miracles and testimonies of how this would turn around. I saw myself braiding her hair, buying the cutest and most comfortable gowns, bringing her breakfast, and taking the best care of her.

Despite a flight delay, Joseph and I arrived in Nashville about an hour past our scheduled arrival time of 4 p.m. and took a taxi to Summit Hospital. As we pulled up to the hospital, my brothers came outside to help with our bags. It was at that moment my entire world collapsed, "She's gone," my brother said. I've never felt pain like I did that day.

I'm not sure there's anything that could've prepared me for this moment. In the days, weeks, and months following, I experienced every emotion possible, and a kind of pain that is still indescribable. At the same time, I channeled my flight and freeze responses to power through planning a legacy celebration for my mother. I helped my dad transition and responded to constant calls and guests, and considered if, how, or when I would return to New York. Whether it was the grief associated with the lack of trust toward my manager or the traumatic loss of my mother while I worked to prove I belonged, getting out of survival mode meant I first had to acknowledge that's where I was.

When we operate in survival mode, we might try to compartmentalize our lives to cope. I tried hard to contain my frustration and anxiety towards my manager and to keep those feelings on the fourth floor of our headquarters on E 42nd Street. The fact of the matter is those feelings traveled home with me from midtown Manhattan to the Upper East Side and into our quaint one-bedroom apartment. I handled my mother's funeral and business affairs with my dad pretty well for a while. But eventually, that dam broke, and my grief nearly swallowed me up.

> *Living in survival mode isn't sustainable. We must reveal our grief to heal.*

Living in survival mode isn't sustainable. We must reveal our grief to heal. Grief—the loss of a routine, experience, expectation, or person—can trigger survival mode. It is complex and hard to journey through but, if we don't sit with our grief and unpack it, we will become immobilized by it. This requires us to sit our pride and fear to the side to reveal where we are. We must be mindful not to make survival mode our permanent residence. It isn't sustainable for our wellness. Here are some signs that you may be in survival mode:

- Mental or physical fatigue
- Mental fog, trouble remembering, or lack of focus
- Neglecting your basic needs or regular daily routine
- Responding more emotionally than usual at home or work
- Isolation or difficulty being social with people in your circle
- Prolonged lack of interest in re-establishing new priorities and routines

If you start to notice these behaviors becoming more commonplace for you than usual, it could be a sign you're in survival mode.

CAN I GRIEVE? BLACK WOMEN AND OUR CAPES

Survival mode has been a way of life for Black Americans since slavery. We are well acquainted with grief, and even our cultural song of resilience by James Weldon Johnson, "Lift Every Voice and Sing," echoes this acknowledgment:

Stony the road we trod,
Bitter the chastening rod,
Felt in the days when hope unborn had died;
Yet with a steady beat,
Have not our weary feet
Come to the place for which our fathers sighed?
We have come over a way that with tears has been watered,
We have come, treading our path through the blood of the slaughtered,
Out from the gloomy past,
Till now we stand at last
Where the white gleam of our bright star is cast.

God of our weary years,
God of our silent tears,
Thou who has brought us thus far on the way;
Thou who has by Thy might Led us into the light,
Keep us forever in the path, we pray.
Lest our feet stray from the places, our God, where we met Thee,
Lest, our hearts drunk with the wine of the world, we forget Thee;
Shadowed beneath Thy hand,
May we forever stand.

True to our God,
True to our native land.[7]

Living with weary years and silent tears due to poverty, mass incarceration, racism, the school-to-prison pipeline, police brutality, and health inequities, to name a few, has left us struggling with cultural baggage that many of us don't know how to unpack healthily. We wear the mask and cape of the Strong Black Woman as a badge of honor and identity. Meanwhile, this identity keeps us suffering in silence and suppressing the natural need to grieve without the fear of judgment or shame. Even amid individual and collective grief that brings us to our knees, there's an unspoken yet widely known expectation to get over it as soon as possible because, well, we're strong! We think, "Look at what our ancestors overcame. This is nothing in comparison!" This self-sabotaging paradigm and Black Superwoman complex is harming us more than we realize. It is imperative for Black people and our allies to create brave spaces to express the individual and collective grief we feel.

> *It is imperative for Black people and our allies to create brave spaces to express the individual and collective grief we feel.*

This collective awareness of the need to make space to grieve and lose our capes starts with us. As women, we must know our lives and businesses aren't validated by how much pain we can survive to

---

[7] James Weldon Johnson. "NAACP History: Lift Every Voice and Sing." NAACP, https://www.naacp.org/naacp-history-lift-evry-voice-and-sing/

prove we're strong. Take off your mask and acknowledge that revealing where you are is essential to healing the pain you suppress. This may mean you can no longer be who you've been for other people as you care and cultivate who you're becoming. My mother's death changed me. I'm not the woman I was before June 5, 2017, and I had to acknowledge this and be my own advocate to honor the changes taking place in me and its impact on those around me. Take the time and create the space you need to breathe and grieve and to deal and heal.

> *Take off your mask and acknowledge that revealing where you are is essential to healing the pain you suppress.*

SAY YES AND ALLOW YOURSELF TO BE SEEN

"Vulnerability is not winning or losing; it's having the courage to show up and be seen when we have no control over the outcome. Vulnerability is not weakness; it's our greatest measure of courage." – Brené Brown

As leaders, often it seems we don't acknowledge the intersectional dynamic embedded in the challenge of vulnerability, particularly for Black women. My friend, Dr. Jessica Williams, wrote about this in her beautiful article titled, "Vulnerability in Black Skin."[8]

---

[8] Jessica Williams. "Vulnerability in Black Skin." http://www.jessicajamese.com/sincerelyjessblog/2020/6/30/cquw6repkxk7y0f8vetjyqejo215kp

> *"I was wrestling with embracing vulnerability within my Black skin. I believed so deeply in the work to be authentic, and to reduce shame, and yet so much around me informed me of the danger in doing so."*

In my own experience, because I've been raised and conditioned by culture to be a strong Black woman and take on this superwomen approach to life, I didn't know how to reveal so I could deal and heal. I still work to be intentional with this. It's as if there isn't time or space to express the depth of pain, fear, loss, anger, disappointment, hurt, etc., for fear of being stereotyped or stepped on or over.

We must give ourselves the grace to reveal how we feel — without judgment— and without apology. I mean saying these things out loud, writing them out, so we hear ourselves say them and then sharing with others. This isn't about people being in our business or being reluctant about (as my mom would say) "keeping house business, house business" but rather about two simple words: self-care. What do you need to operate as your highest self? Perhaps it's not another bag, spa day, sneaker release purchase, candle, or manicure we need. Instead, maybe it's time to substitute our retail therapy for a regular therapy appointment with a licensed professional to help us reveal where we are so we can deal and then heal. My hope for you is that you will rest your cape and give yourself permission to be seen, to thrive authentically, and to do this on your own terms!

> *We must give ourselves the grace to reveal how we feel —without judgment— and without apology.*

Thoughts along the journey:

3. Reveal and Deal

Complete the journal prompt.

I need to be more open about:

_____
_____
_____
_____
_____
_____
_____
_____
_____
_____
_____
_____
_____

To support my journey to be more transparent about where I am, I will:

CHAPTER 4

Don't Should Yourself

Time passes; it doesn't heal. Reveal and deal to heal.

When was the last time you were uncomfortable? Think about it. Where were you? What were you doing? Who was with you? What exactly made you uncomfortable? Being in a season of transition can bring about a series of painful moments. Currently, amid Covid-19, I've found myself in a constant state of uncomfortable moments that aren't what I expected or planned. In the first chapter, we discussed how grief is one of the most complex and unpredictable emotions we experience in response to a loss. This loss can be tangible or intangible. Perhaps you are a high achiever, a leader, proactive, and someone who embodies discipline. Whether we're employed and doing meaningful work at an organization that aligns with our values or we're entrepreneurs leading organizations based on our values; discipline is essential for thriving professionals. It's the common thread that allows us to make progress in the successful pursuit of our goals. If you're someone who values discipline, then inherently, you also value consistency.

> *Discipline is essential for thriving professionals.*

Discipline is built on this idea that regardless of what is happening around us or in us, we can engage in consistent action to create habits to reach our goals. Let's take working out, for example. I've always been an athlete. Now maybe not a Division 1 college athlete or professional athlete, but from elementary school junior pro to high school varsity and AAU I was on the basketball team; and during my junior pro days I was the only girl. It took countless hours of practice to build up my skills to move from only getting in when the team had a big lead to being a starter. These early moments of playing AAU basketball, volleyball, and track built up my discipline and confidence. I learned that if you're committed to the consistency of practice and hard work, you can, in many ways, control the outcome. While this may be the case with athletes or sports or even high business performance, it is often not the case with grief.

One of the things grief has taught me is how much I am not in control. Regardless of how disciplined I am, irrespective of how much grit I exude to get to this ideal place or reach this goal, grief flies in the face of every measure of discipline or self-control I possess. Now, as a Type A personality, it can be tough to surrender control. If you're like me and are more D on the DISC assessment scale (Dominance, Influence, Steadiness, and Conscientiousness), we value having a sense of self-control. It's why many professionals leap into entrepreneurship because they want to control their destiny. Many of us want to be able to manage our income. We want to be able to control who our colleagues are. While these preferences could help us in many areas of life, maintaining control often is counterproductive to navigating our grief journey with real resilience.

BALANCING GRIT AND GRACE

Counterproductive? Yes, because perhaps in our effort to maintain control to be disciplined in our response to a profound loss, we get comfortable wearing a mask to cover how we feel. The book, The Grief Recovery Handbook by John W. James and Russell Friedman, founders of the Grief Recovery Institute, talks about "the Academy Award recovery" and how society teaches us how to act recovered. We put on a happy face when people ask how we're doing and say we're fine. We project feelings of "strength" to maintain control. Much of how we respond to grief comes from an intellectual place instead of an emotional place. We give head responses and not heart responses. And many times, "I'm fine" is a lie.

I've never felt more out of control than returning to New York after my mother's death. For months I wrestled with my inability to be able to control my emotions. Whether I was sitting in my office on a call with an agency partner, walking to the subway, sitting in our apartment, or getting in a taxi to head to the airport, I would experience sadness and tears that would come out of nowhere. In many of those moments, it wasn't "the right time." This gripping nature of grief left me feeling bewildered by my inability to control how I was feeling. As many of us know, when you're struggling with the loss, you never know when a memory, a moment, or a smell will trigger a reminder that sends you spiraling emotionally. In these moments,

> *One of the ways we give ourselves grace is by giving ourselves permission to fully experience this new place.*

I've learned to leave grit to the business and the professional career and give myself the grace to fully experience every feeling of grief. To surrender control of how I wish to feel or the strength I'd like to project and allow my emotions to be. One of the ways we give ourselves grace is by giving ourselves permission to fully experience this new place.

NEVER EXPERIENCED ANYTHING LIKE THIS

Let's revisit this critical question: When was the last time you were uncomfortable? What memory comes to mind? Was it uncomfortable because it was hard? Or because you didn't want to do it? Or were you uncomfortable because the task was complex? Or perhaps was it uncomfortable because it was a new experience?

When we get to the core of why these are our most uncomfortable moments, for many of us our discomfort is connected to the newness of the experience. We're uncomfortable because we've never had a conversation about this topic with this person. Or we've never had to challenge this person on this topic. We've never been confronted with these thoughts or feelings. Whatever the case may be, experiencing new moments, new conversations, new people, and even new emotions are invitations to give ourselves the grace to feel through the moment instead of trying to block out or box in how we "should" respond to the moment. In addition to the new experiences and feelings, there are those instances, particularly with the loss of a loved one, where we just don't have the space to have this emotional response right now. There have been times when I was about to go to a meeting where I had to present, and a moment entered my mind and conjured up emotions I didn't have time for. I've learned this valuable approach of thought stopping. We'll talk more about thought stopping and how to take your thoughts captive later in this chapter. Let's acknowledge that we all have moments like this, where we need to push past our present feelings to "get the job done." However, let's ensure they are moments, and even rare moments, rather than how we cope to come across as "strong."

I want to invite us to feel through moments that are new to us. When we experience change, challenge, and loss, it disrupts our routine and expectations. Those realities create a new territory for us—places we've never experienced before and often could not have predicted or chosen for ourselves. Due to this, I've had to unlearn my natural response to place unrealistic expectations on myself, compartmentalize my emotions, try to maintain control of the outcome, and have a perfect answer to unexpected, life-altering moments.

> *I've had to unlearn my natural response to place unrealistic expectations on myself, compartmentalize my emotions, try to maintain control of the outcome, and have a perfect answer to unexpected, life-altering moments.*

THEY CAN'T SAY HOW YOU SHOULD FEEL

Part of what amplifies our tendency to be in control and mask our genuine response to a loss isn't only our expectations but the expectations of others. Most of us are not prepared to help others through a season of grief and loss. The responses and opinions of friends, colleagues, and family members of grieving individuals can add to this already natural tendency to should ourselves through our process. We don't make space for how we feel because we're always judging and being judged by some arbitrary standard or misinterpreted scripture of how we should feel. When we hear that someone has experienced the loss of a loved one, marriage, job, etc., we typically don't know what to say. One of the first things we often do is mirror what we hear through the lens of our own lived experiences. For example, when we hear someone has faced a loss, we naturally try to find a common thread in our own lives to express sympathy. But here's the thing, sympathy is not empathy.

Most people need our empathy, not our sympathy. Empathy is about the other person. Empathy is not about you. The moment we respond to someone else's grief through the lens of our own lived experience, we make the conversation and his or her experience about us, even in the affirmative. We put up a mirror of comparing how that other person should feel based on our response to the similar loss we experienced. This can be subtle and such a habit that we don't even recognize we're doing it.

> *Most people need our empathy, not our sympathy. Empathy is about the other person. Empathy is not about you.*

One of the worst things to say after someone experienced a loss is, "I know how you feel" or "I understand." In the early months after my mother's death, these were two of the statements that would make the hairs on the back of my neck stand up. I rarely responded to the sentiment when people would say this, but often I was incredibly annoyed by these statements as the individual didn't know how I felt or even bother to ask. My relationship with my mother was unique. Even my brothers and dad didn't fully understand my grief because my relationship and experiences with my mother were mine. We had moments together that only we shared, so my experience grieving her is also unique. John James and Russell Freedman, renowned grief experts and authors of The Grief Recovery Handbook, share profound examples of how we must be intentional to not allow intellectual connections to overpower emotional truths. Whether it's the intellectual analysis of relationships, scientific facts related to health, or even faith, it's essential to create space for the reality of our emotions. Your relationships are unique, and so is your grief.

Another inadequate response is changing the subject after someone shares his or her pain. I know. I know. Who would do such a thing? That sounds rude, right? Well, it happens often and mostly unintentionally. How does this look? A few weeks after my mother's death, my godson, a week after his first birthday, passed away from a rare form of cancer. Attending his funeral with his mom and dad was one of the most challenging moments of my life. I remember well-meaning family and friends making statements starting with "at least," and again, the hairs on the back of my neck would stand up. We change the subject when we say these things: "Well, at least they lived to be X years old;" or "At least they're not in pain anymore;" or "At least you were able to spend time with them and say your goodbyes before they passed;" or "At least you had a great experience, and you were in a good role. You can find another job." The moment we use this type of language unwittingly or not, we change the subject and dismiss how the person is feeling. When we respond in this way, we don't create space for how people genuinely experience their grief. Instead, we put up this mirror for how they should feel and how they should think. Don't should yourself and don't allow others to should you!

In the space below, take some time to write out how you feel. We are either in transition, we just came out of one, or we're moving closer to our next shift. It makes no difference whether they are transitions we chose or transitions that chose us. We inevitably leave something behind when we step into something new. When changes take place, there is a sense of loss. I hope as you're reading this, you're becoming more aware of how and when to create space and grace to grieve. I want you also to create space to acknowledge how you feel.

We did this in chapter one, but I want to leave some room here as well. Take a few moments and think about either your current transition, the transition you just came out of, or your transition that may be down the road. How do you feel about it? What are your thoughts? What emotions do you have? This section below is your space in your book to be completely honest with yourself. There are no wrong or right answers. This is your opportunity to express your feelings in writing without judgment. There is no specific way you are supposed to respond other than how you feel right now, at this moment. Go ahead. Grab a pen and take a few moments to write out how you feel. It can be in sentences, words, bullet points, pictures, etc. There is no judgment and no rules for how to express your feelings below.

When I think about _____
(insert transition, challenge or loss) I feel...

_____
_____
_____
_____
_____
_____
_____
_____
_____
_____
_____
_____
_____

FEELING AND KNOWING

It was an out of body experience. I was sitting on an antique, floral-patterned couch next to an old maple wood colored desk with a catalog of coffins in my lap. As I turned the page and asked my brother which one, I sat there thinking, "Am I really doing this? Am I really picking out a coffin for my mother?" It was unlike anything I had ever encountered before. And at the same time, it was familiar. I knew what it meant to have a goal and a deadline and to tap into go mode to reach the goal by the deadline. Administration and planning come naturally to me, and in many ways, this felt like I was planning and prioritizing as I had done before. I remember having this highly organized, thorough, and structured approach. I knew what needed to come next and learned how to get it done even though I had never experienced this before. I was in my zone. Then the moment hit me. As I was making plans and positioning the right people to help, it hit me and I completely collapsed... literally.

    I was in Dillard's in Green Hills Mall in Nashville with my sister-in-love, godmother, and best friend. My brother shared his only request throughout her funeral planning—for me to go to the mall and buy our mom a new suit instead of picking something out of her closet. New suit? I added it to the list. Since the funeral home needed it the next day, we hopped in the car and drove across town to get it done. As we stepped out of the car in the parking garage and opened up the door to the escalators to enter the mall, I took about four steps, and it all hit me. It was as if Floyd Mayweather had just punched me in the gut, and my knees buckled. I was going in one of our favorite stores to pick out the final outfit my mother would ever wear. In all of the many moments, I had dressed her, shopped for her, went shopping with her, given her tips on what would look good (even though she needed none and taught me everything I knew about style), this would be the last moment I would get to do this for her. Thankfully a bench was there to break up my fall, and so were my best friend, my sister-in-love, and my godmother, who comforted me and helped me somehow make it upstairs to the women's section to pick out the most beautiful coral suit I just knew my mom would have loved.

In this moment and countless times in the days, weeks, months, and years that followed, I had to learn how to navigate the contradicting balance of what I feel and what I know. Our awareness and acknowledgment of our feelings lead us to heal adequately. It reveals our raw and transparent emotion, and this is where we learn to deal with how we feel so we can start to heal. Many of us hide our feelings because we think it means we're allowing our emotions to control us. We remain guarded, wear the mask, and fake being fine to stay in control of our words and actions. However, when we are vulnerable about where we are and the emotions tied to that place, we open the door for growth and healing to take place. So, if you skipped over the previous section to write down your feelings, I encourage you to go back and use it. You can acknowledge how you honestly feel and, by revealing where you are, demonstrate the faith and fortitude to journey through those feelings to wholeness and healing.

What do we do when our feelings overshadow what we know? For many of us, moments like this can trigger a tug-of-war between our faith and our feelings. In my faith as a Christian, we're taught that our faith takes precedence over feelings. As a result, many of us believe and have faith beyond reason and despite facts. The entire meaning of having faith is for us to have deep confidence and persuasion in an outcome we cannot see. For some reason, this is what God laid on my heart when I spoke at my mother's funeral – how do we journey forward when our feelings are in polarizing opposition with our faith. I still have the notes in my phone I typed that day in the family car heading to the funeral.

I learned to give myself the space to acknowledge my emotions by reminding myself of what I already know. I call this dealing and healing, feeling, and knowing. I used to think of this as feeling versus knowing, but the two can coexist in actuality. From picking out a coffin on the couch to the last time I styled my mom in a look she would love, I realized I don't have to wear a cape and pretend not to feel the way I do. You don't have to apply the mask so you can be seen as strong. Give yourself permission to acknowledge every emotion you're feeling and remind yourself of what you know, especially when you're not feeling it. Transforming our feelings comes through how we choose to renew our minds. It's hard to know what needs to be transformed when we're hiding how we feel. Make space for how you feel while also affirming out loud what you know. One of the ways you can do this is by taking your thoughts captive. Before we talk about that, though, we must discuss the dreaded G-word.

> *Give yourself permission to acknowledge every emotion you're feeling and remind yourself of what you know, especially when you're not feeling it.*

RELEASE YOURSELF FROM THE GUILT

We always say hindsight is 20/20. Guess what grief does? It catapults you into living your days in retrospect. When we experience deep loss, we almost unconsciously start to think back to the moments before the loss happened. We recall our fondest memories; moments we shared; experiences we had; and places we went. If you've experienced the death of loved ones, then you know exactly how this looks. You almost immediately think back to the last time you spoke with them, heard from them, or were with them. You try to recall the last conversation and what you said. If it's an unexpected death, you ask yourself if there were signs you missed. You question why you didn't notice this would happen or why you made those last few decisions. You think about the last time you spent time in each other's presence. You search your phone, laptop, or cloud storage for pictures of them to recall memories of moments you shared. As we're inundated with these flashback memories, perhaps we notice things we didn't recognize in real-time. We start to recall things we wish were different: conversations we wished we'd had or something we wish we hadn't said. If we aren't careful, we can drown ourselves in what-ifs and should-haves.

    I know this because I've had many of these same moments. I questioned why I didn't fly to Nashville the weekend of June 2, 2017. My mom's best friend from college and her daughter came to Nashville from Charleston (my mom's hometown) to visit her. The four of us had a tradition of taking a mother/daughter trip every year for many years. Many of my fond memories with my mother are from these trips. My favorite trip was our extended girls' trip from Las Vegas to Los Angeles. We had a blast that year. When my mom's friend learned about her health, she made plans to visit her with her daughter. I was living in New York and had bought a ticket to see my mom the following weekend.

    For days, I debated the decision whether or not to come home back-to-back weekends. Joseph and I talked about all the angles. I had every-other-weekend trips booked and planned to take several months off for her surgery later that summer. I also thought about the financial implications. Our cash flow was extremely tight during this time. We were still paying a mortgage in Chattanooga, paying rent for our NYC apartment that was more than twice our mortgage, and flying home to Nashville every other weekend to see my mom. I decided not to fly home that weekend, and that was my mom's last weekend alive. My eyes are filled with tears even as I share this with you at this moment because I know the weight of "why didn't I make a different decision." Why didn't I just put the flight on a credit card and hang out with my mom, her best friend, and her daughter the way we had in so many other cities on our countless girls' trips. I would've been with her Sunday night instead of just on the phone watching Lebron James and the Cavs together. I would've been present early Monday morning when my dad realized she wasn't breathing in bed next to him. The guilt of this decision has anchored me in despair for years. It wasn't until a random day I was released from the weight of this guilt on a seemingly random Instagram Live. Can I share that story with you?

Thasunda Brown Duckett is the Chief Executive Officer of Chase Consumer Banking, a division of JP Morgan, and recognized by Fortune and many others as one of the world's most powerful women. I had the pleasure of meeting Thasunda at an executive leadership luncheon with the Nashville Chamber of Commerce and not only is she one of the most brilliant women I've ever met, but she's also a Black woman who is so authentic and unapologetic about her heritage! I remember feeling so proud and inspired sitting on the front row of her talk as she shared her experiences as a Black woman in corporate America from the stage (in a room with a mostly white audience) as if we were on the phone in our pajamas with a glass of wine having girl talk. I'd never witnessed a corporate executive leader—particularly a Black woman—be so charismatic, transparent, inspiring, approachable and genuine all at the same time. She's real salt and light seated in high places, and it's beautiful to witness! So, of course, I followed her everywhere on social media. A few months later, she launched this Instagram Live series on "When Purpose Introduced Herself." Each live session had a different topic, and once it ended, she would always do an after-show where she would invite viewers to join her on camera during the live afterparty talk. I had joined a couple of these before as a listener, learning vicariously through those that joined her live to share. She made a simple request. "Take a deep breath and forgive yourself." Y'all, I don't know what came over me this particular day. Well, yes, I do. It was the Holy Spirit. Before I knew it, I'd pressed the button to join her live.

> *"Take a deep breath and forgive yourself."*

I had no idea what I was going to say. My heart was pounding. As soon as she welcomed me on, all the nervousness went away, and I just started sharing. Long story short, I cried an ugly cry on Thasunda's Instagram Live with hundreds of women watching. (*insert scream* I am not a public crier! It's the first rule of professional womanhood: Corporate women don't cry, right? Wrong.) It was the most unexpected yet freeing moment I've ever experienced around my mother's death. I want to share with you what she shared with me on this day, May 20, 2020, and I hope it releases you too:

> *"I made the best decision with the faculties I was given. If I had been given different faculties, I would've made a different decision. I'm taking a deep breath, and I forgive myself."*

Thasunda was so gracious encouraging me and sharing her wisdom that day. I'll always remember this weight-lifting moment that helped my guilt shift to grace. Forgiving yourself can be harder than forgiving others, and this was the day I began to give myself grace for not being there when my mom died.

My family has always been a priority over my career. My mom knew that. She was my chief cheerleader encouraging me to take the New York position—the one tailored made for me after turning down the first opportunity and working so hard to prove I belonged at the table. I remember calling her when I got the offer and her celebrating me with, "You see how God works things out? His timing is perfect." She knew how hard I'd worked to get this opportunity again. Also, she knew I loved her, and even though she may have withheld the details of her prognosis from me (another source of the anger around my grief), even that decision was based on her love and our beautiful bond. I forgive her, and I forgive myself for not being there when she took her last breath. That, too, was God's plan. I rest in knowing His ways are better than mine, and His thoughts are higher than mine. I'm taking a breath, and I've forgiven myself.

Now, what do you need to forgive yourself for? I wasn't expecting this breakthrough and release of guilt to come in this way. But I'm so grateful for Thasunda and her divine alignment in a moment that I didn't even know I needed. Part of navigating through our grief and releasing

> *I've learned it takes discipline to be aware of our thoughts and assess which ones to take action on and which ones to replace with a better thought.*

ourselves from the guilt is being open to moments we least expect. Changing what we believe is hard and sometimes the transformation we need comes in unexpected moments. I've learned it takes discipline to be aware of our thoughts and assess which ones to take action on and which ones to replace with a better thought. Let's briefly discuss how we can take our thoughts captive in ways that will help us to stop "shoulding" ourselves.

TAKING YOUR THOUGHTS CAPTIVE

How do you develop mental toughness? One practice you could implement to help shape a growth mindset and resilience is assessing your thoughts. Thought stopping has become a technique that has helped me become more self-aware. When we are more aware of what we think, we can start to make shifts in how we think. Those shifts in how we think will ultimately help us to navigate the way we feel. Clinical psychologist Carla Marie Manly, Ph.D., and author of Joy from Fear, teaches how thought stopping is a traditional cognitive-behavioral technique designed to replace the negative or unwanted thought with a more positive or neutral one.[9] This clinical behavioral therapy of thought-stopping is also aligned with the Biblical principle of taking your thoughts captive in 2 Corinthians 10:5. Although we may be familiar with this language, how to do this is rarely really explained.

> *When we are more aware of what we think, we can start to make shifts in how we think.*

---

[9] Carla Marie Manly. Joy from Fear: Create the Life of Your Dreams by Making Fear Your Friend (Familius, 2019)

Taking my thoughts captive has been an essential element of creating a deeper level of self-awareness that helps me deal to heal. Below I want to share with you an acronym I use to take my thoughts **C.A.P.T.I.V.E.**

CHALLENGE – Challenge your thoughts by interrupting them and asking yourself one of the most powerful self-awareness questions: "Why do I think that?" Do you think this way because of something you've experienced? Is it a fear-based thought that has never actually happened? Is it a thought based on something you have read or a vicarious experience of someone you know? Don't just suppress your thoughts; challenge them to uncover why you're thinking this way. Could it be an experience from your childhood creating the story you're telling yourself? Interrogate the thought by asking why do I believe that.

AWARENESS – Challenging your thoughts will help you to become more aware of them and their source next time. Often when we have thoughts, particularly ones we define as "sad" or "negative," we just kind of let them go. Instead, we want to increase our awareness of what and how we're thinking to apply the next step.

PERSIST – Persisting is about shifting your energy, which requires fortitude. Persisting isn't about going around it or suppressing it. Instead, when you push through the thought, you're more likely to develop the mental toughness and skill to replace ideas that are counterproductive with new affirmations of the truth.

TRUTH – When we decide a thought or belief no longer serves us, it's essential to put something else in its place. In taking your thoughts captive, you want to replace the negative thinking with the truth. Use affirmations, Scripture, quotes, etc., to replace negative thinking with an idea that is steeped in the truth. This step also requires us to be aware of the truth we're taking in to replace negative thoughts. Assess the content you ingest to ensure you have a catalog of truth to use. For example, your social media feed does just that – it feeds you. Be aware of what you listen to, read, and watch to ensure you're taking in sources of truth.

INTENTION – Focus in on your vision. One of my favorite Scripture passages is this picture of Jesus, who had such an incredible vision of what was to come despite being nailed to a cross. The vision helped Him to withstand what was presently happening. Hebrews 12:2 says, "Looking to Jesus the founder and perfecter of our faith, who for the joy that was set before him endured the cross, despising the shame, and is seated at the right hand of the throne of God" (ESV). What picture of joy are you envisioning to fix your focus forward? How are you being intentional with your focus?

VISION – Setting an intention helps us to create a vision to see ourselves the way we want to be. Create a vision for your life to help to guide your intentions. When you wake up in the morning or the middle of the day or before you go to bed at night, spend some time visualizing where it is you want to be in every area of your life—personally, professionally, health-wise, financially, etc. Make the time to see yourself the way you want to be. Part of becoming the best version of ourselves is having a vision of what that looks like and choosing to believe it.

EVERYDAY – Oh, you thought this was one and done? Nope. We must repeat these strategies daily or until they become habits for how we guard our thoughts. This isn't a one-and-done process. Rather, through daily repetition, this becomes how we develop our mental resilience to take our thoughts captive while we give ourselves space to feel. As we take our thoughts captive and renew our minds, we eventually transform how we feel. For more on this topic of taking your thoughts captive, check out the Career Thrivers Podcast, Episode Five. I recorded an entire episode on Taking Your Thoughts Captive. You can access it by subscribing to the podcast on iTunes, Spotify, or wherever you listen to podcasts. Or go to brittanyncole.com/podcast to access this episode.

NOW LET'S AFFIRM THIS:

> *I am equipped to thrive through my current challenges. Everything I need is within me. Obstacles are an opportunity to reimagine and re-create in unprecedented ways. I am aware of my thoughts and will maintain my peace of mind in challenging situations today. I was built for this. I control what I choose to focus on today, and I will replace negative thoughts with thoughts that are true, pure, lovely, and good. I am a thriver.*

Most of us aren't taught, prepped, or guided on grief until we're experiencing it. We have the Lamaze Method for soon to be parents and pre-marital counseling for soon to be spouses, but the actual event is usually our first teacher on grief. Therefore, allow yourself the space to respond in new ways because, in many ways, most of what you're experiencing is new to you. It's okay not to be strong. We don't have to pretend we're strong to show we're brave, worthy, or capable. Release yourself from the expectations of others and even the ones you're placing on yourself. Notice what moves you and lean into those feelings while giving yourself the grace to learn, unlearn, and relearn where you are now. Tell yourself a new story as you rewrite the script for your life. Remove the cape. Be present. Stay purposeful. Take your thoughts captive. Stop "shoulding" yourself. Take a deep breath. And forgive yourself.

Thoughts along the journey:

4. Be Okay with Being Uncomfortable

Discomfort is the perfect opportunity for growth. How can you embrace being more comfortable with feelings of discomfort?

1. What are you feeling?

2. What is inside your comfort zone? What is outside your comfort zone?

3. Choose one thing that makes you uncomfortable and make a plan to share it with someone. Set a date and decide the person you will share with. Write them both below.

4. Now that you have some accountability, set a date for when you will do it! Get comfortable taking action beyond your comfort zone; that's where growth happens!

WHAT'S INSIDE YOUR *Comfort Zone?*

WHAT MAKES YOU *Uncomfortable?*

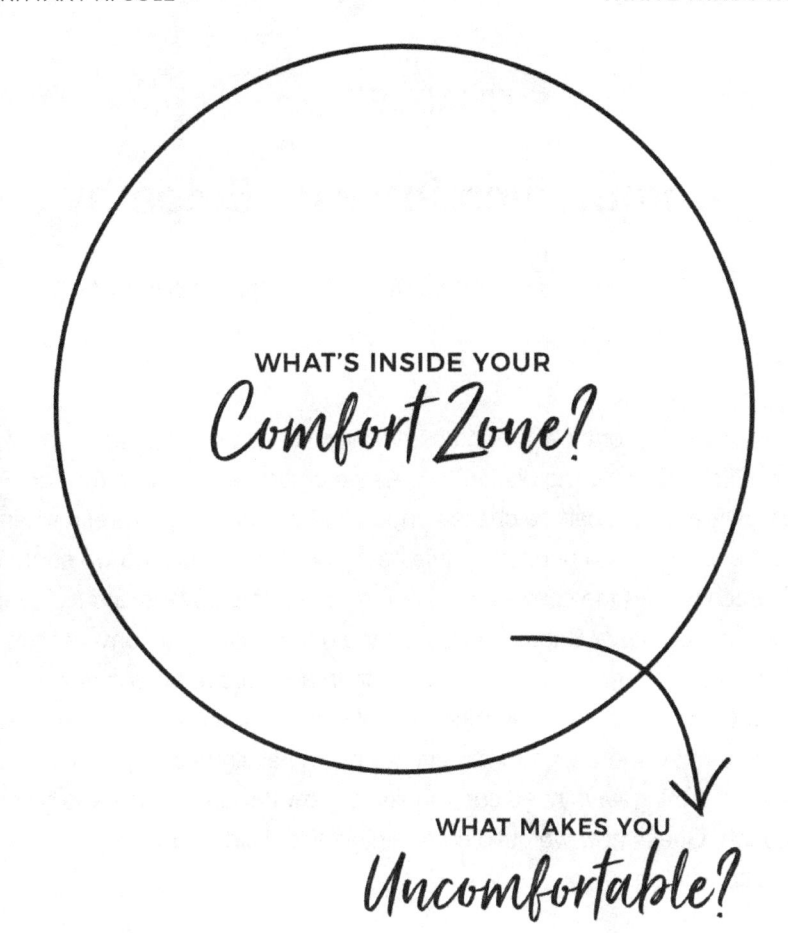

CHAPTER 5

Communicating with Empathy

How do you communicate through the discomfort?

Our uncertainty around communication is usually at the core of our difficulty embracing discomfort. As we embrace a deeper level of self-awareness, it can be challenging to find the words to express where we are as we're still unpacking this new place. How much do we share? How do we start the conversation before more time passes and it's even more complicated? Shouldn't they be the ones initiating a conversation? There are often many more questions than answers regarding how to communicate with others in moments of change and loss. It can feel like it's better to withdraw and wait until we have it all figured out. However, here's the thing—we need community to grow through what we're going through. Guess how we build community? We build it through communication.

THE CHALLENGES WITH HARD CONVERSATIONS

Any obstacle I have overcome has been in large part because of the support of other people. Having a healthy support system is essential as you're navigating through change, challenge, and loss. Part of the

> *Part of the strength of that support system relies on our ability to communicate with them in a meaningful way during challenging moments.*

strength of that support system relies on our ability to communicate with them in a meaningful way during challenging moments. Often this means having tough conversations. You know the ones, those conversations that take us weeks, months, and even years to have. Perhaps these conversations haven't happened yet because we don't know where to start or what to say. It can be a catch-22 because as you're debating over what to say, when, and how, time is passing, making it even more difficult to navigate what to say.

WHAT EXACTLY MAKES THESE CONVERSATIONS SO HARD?

EMOTIONS

In many contexts, we're conditioned not to deal with our emotions. For example, in professional settings, we often hear things like there's no room for emotion, and we try to approach the conversation in an emotionless way. The opposite end of the spectrum may also be true. Perhaps you've witnessed a moment where emotions completely took over and caused reactions based upon someone's feelings versus the person responding with a priority to connect effectively. Emotional intelligence becomes so critical to communicating through the discomfort.

Effective communication includes **three main components:**

**our capacity to be aware of how we feel,
our ability to effectively express ourselves, and
our capability to acknowledge others' emotions and thoughts.**

TIMING

Timing also creates a challenge. Often the conversations we need to have the most happen well after the change, challenge, or loss. Is there ever a right time to have an uncomfortable conversation? Between the initial discomfort, needing time to process our emotions, and the uncertainty of how to have the conversation, we delay it. We don't prioritize the conversation despite the discomfort. We try to get over it instead of addressing and navigating through it. Although you may need to take time to process, keep in mind that timing alone doesn't make the process easier. As we're journeying through and thinking about our healing process, we must acknowledge that the healing on the other side of loss is found only in doing the work. We must deal to heal. Having the tough conversations and asking the hard questions we don't want to hear the answers to are all part of doing the work to thrive through loss.

KNOW-HOW

Once you've processed your emotions and found the right time to talk, what do you say? This alone can be a barrier delaying the conversation even further. We rack our brains, trying to figure out what to say. What are the right words? How do you articulate what you're feeling? Will your honesty offend? Later in this chapter, I will share a framework I created called **Empathy Conversations** to help us understand how to communicate through emotionally charged discomfort.

COMMUNICATING TO BUILD CONNECTION

Whether you're looking to exchange information, solve a problem, entertain, persuade, lead, motivate, or establish goals, the common thread amongst any purpose of communication is connection. To reach the intended goal of communication, we must first connect with the listener. The connection is the goal of any productive communication. The conversation isn't the goal— connection is. When we shift our mindset around this, it changes how we approach challenging conversations. We focus less on the content and more on the connection. The conversation is a tool to reach the ultimate goal of a relationship. Regardless of if

> *The connection is the goal of any productive communication. The conversation isn't the goal— connection is.*

you're communicating through discomfort with a colleague, family member, client, or friend, spend some time thinking through how you want to connect with the person and then focus on what you want to say. In his book, Everyone Communicates, Few Connect, John C. Maxwell shares that connecting is never about us. It's about the person we're communicating with to cultivate connection.[10]

In essence, our conversations with others are meant to center the people we're in communication with—not ourselves. It's not about you—it's about them. If you want to connect with others, you must get over yourself to understand and connect with other people's thoughts, beliefs, and experiences. This is what it means to communicate with empathy. We will talk more about what this looks like later in this chapter.

After getting over ourselves, we must get a clue. I mean this more figuratively than literally. A. **C.L.U.E.** is an acronym for how to prioritize connection as we communicate with others. Let's briefly walk through ways to get a clue and communicate to connect.

A CLUE for Prioritizing Connection in Communication

AWARENESS – One way to build connection through communication is to prioritize learning more about the person we're speaking with and gaining more awareness on the topic. Instead of focusing only on the content we want to share, we focus on our self and social awareness to manage our relationships through the conversation. Are there things about this person's experiences you can learn? Do you know the person's current challenges? Are you aware of why the person hasn't reached out to have a conversation with you? Enter the discussion with the assumption there's more for you to learn to raise your awareness through the exchange.

---

[10] Maxwell, J. C. (2010). Everyone Communicates, Few Connect. Thomas Nelson.

CLARITY – Seeking clarity on the other person's thoughts and feelings helps us increase connection and emotional intelligence in our communication. We want to be as transparent as possible in our conversation. This may mean we ask more questions than we make statements then summarize what we've heard to ensure we're aligned. Additionally, thinking through one thing we want to know more about from the other person's perspective will help us gain clarity and set us up to enter the conversation ready to listen, learn, and empathize.

LISTEN – We build this clarity through listening. We've heard the adage that "we have two ears and one mouth so that we can listen twice as much as we speak." I agree with this and would add that active listening is a skill. We aren't listening to formulate a persuasive response; rather, we're listening to understand. How did the person you're communicating with answer the questions to which you wanted more clarity? What is their perspective on the topic? Is it the same or different than what you anticipated?

UNDERSTAND – If we're prioritizing connection in our communication, listening to what's being said and what's not being said helps us understand the other person better. This becomes our foundation for communication to build a connection with others. Here, we have a level of understanding of how the other person is thinking, feeling, and experiencing the shared dialogue.

EMPATHIZE – The more we seek to understand others, the more seamless it is to empathize. Empathy requires us to decenter our thoughts and feelings to step into the thoughts, feelings, and experiences of someone else. We will talk more about the mechanics of empathy conversations in just a moment.

> *Empathy requires us to decenter our thoughts and feelings to step into the thoughts, feelings, and experiences of <u>someone else.</u>*

    I have found these tenets of communication to connect helpful both personally and professionally. Whether we are journeying through a loss or talking with someone who is, getting A CLUE will help us connect with others in a meaningful way. What other ways can we be intentional in our communication and interactions to support someone through change, loss, and transition?

WAYS TO SUPPORT SOMEONE THROUGH GRIEF

    One of the misnomers of grief is that time alone heals all. We think if we give it or them enough time, they will get over it. Time does nothing without doing the work. The healing on the other side of loss is often found through participating in the process—having the tough conversations, asking the hard questions, and being willing to step outside our comfort zone to pray and do the work.

> *The healing on the other side of loss is often found through participating in the process.*

As we discussed earlier, there isn't a one-size-fits-all approach for grief. Being in the circle of support for someone else who is grieving unleashes the desire to bring about resolve. We come into the situation with the intention to provide a solution. We know this is true because just think about the familiar phrase most people express when they initially hear a loved one has died. People often say, "I don't know what to say." Or said another way, "I don't have a solution to offer them. I don't know how to make them feel better." This can keep some of us from reaching out when in actuality, what the person needs most isn't a solution from you or an eloquent statement or tangible gesture. The person likely needs to know you care and know you are there through your presence.

Yes, there are ways to express your condolences tangibly but don't allow that to be at the forefront of how you navigate your interaction with someone who's grieving. The most important thing you can do is to be present. Your presence is appreciated. Often the person who's going through the grief doesn't even know precisely what they need. Therefore, saying things such as, "Let me know what you need," can sometimes fall flat. What I found to be most helpful in the weeks and months after my mother's death were the encouraging texts or calls to check on me; the random messages sharing a memory of my mother; and the photos of her friends and family would share out of the blue which would bring a smile to my face.

Some may think doing this causes a negative response or triggers a sad moment. But I've found it to be quite the opposite. I think about my mother every single day, throughout the day. Acknowledging her memory, her legacy, and her life brings me joy. I always appreciate those moments. Chances are, the people you know who are grieving the loss of a loved one would too. Here are a few additional thoughts on supporting someone who is grieving the loss of a loved one:

MENTION IT – Ignoring the person's loss can feel as if you're ignoring it. Check-in on your colleague, family member, or friend to show you're thinking of them and want to offer support through the person's journey. Here are some things you can say:

> *"Hey, I was just thinking about you. Is there something I can take off of your plate during this time to support you?"*
>
> *"I'm sorry for your loss. I'm here for you if you ever want to talk about it. I want to support you."*
>
> *"I'm covering for you while you're away, so take all the time you need."*
>
> *"You were on my mind today. I know you are hurting. Would you like to talk through how you're feeling today?"*

JUST DO IT – Depending on your relationship with the person who's grieving, you may notice ways you can support without even asking. For example, I have this fantastic group of sister-friends, and we somehow ended up with the name "The Quad": Verlinda, Martina, and Audrienne. I'll always remember I was out of town for work for a week, and at this particular time my mother was in the hospital. I'd shared with them about the upcoming big surgery and how I was trying to balance work to do as much as possible before asking for extended time away. During the week I was out of town, I returned to my hotel room from a long day of meetings and dinner to the most beautiful bouquet they had sent to my room with a thoughtful card. It was such a kind gesture. When my mom died, this same group of friends, although I told them I would get it done, printed off the photo of my mom I wanted to be displayed by her casket, had it framed, and ensured it was delivered to the church the day of her service. They said, "Nope. We're going to take care of that. You focus on something else." Although I thought I could handle it, this was such a breath of fresh air not to worry about getting this task done. I still don't know exactly how they pulled either of these thoughtful gestures off. They just did it.

DON'T FIX IT – One of the worst phrases to say to someone who's grieving is "At least…" Any statement starting with at least, save it. You aren't trying to fix or solve this problem for this person. You can't. It's better to say nothing than to discredit the bereaved person's emotions and belittle the grief by comparing it to anyone or anything else. You can't fix it. Please don't compare the person's grief to anyone else's, including yours.

Surprisingly, one of the most challenging communities to have conversations around grief can be the church. I love the church, but we can say the darndest things trying to solve a problem we can't remedy. Have you ever considered how Jesus communicated with those who were grieving?

A MODEL FOR COMMUNICATING THROUGH DIFFERENCES

I want to spend some time helping those of us who often feel as if we don't know what to do or what to say when someone else is grieving. Specifically, I want to share a Biblical story you may be familiar with—the story of Lazarus. In this biblical account, Lazarus was a sick man who was from a village called Bethany. He had two sisters named Mary and Martha. The sisters sent a message to their good friend, Jesus, letting Him know His friend Lazarus needed him right away. When Jesus received the news, He stayed where He was for two more days. Pause. Yes, you read that right. Upon receiving the news of His good friend's sickness, He didn't immediately rush back. But instead, acknowledged that Lazarus' sickness wouldn't lead to death.

Typically, when this story is shared, the focus is on this next part. When Jesus finally arrived, Lazarus had been dead and buried four days. The moment Mary and Martha saw Jesus, they questioned why He hadn't come sooner because their brother was dead. Although this is a powerful part of the story, and there is so much to extract from these verses, I want to draw your attention to the shortest verse in the Bible in John 11:35. The verse reads, "Jesus wept." The question here is why would Jesus cry when He knew before even going to Bethany, He would raise Lazarus from the dead? How do we respond when we are fully aware of something and interact with someone who doesn't believe or understand what we know? I'll raise my hand.

I'm usually quick to share what I know! Jesus could have easily responded, "Wait. Why are you crying? Do you not know who I am? Dry up those tears and watch what I'm about to do for you!" This may sound extreme because we know how the story ends. However, this sounds like many conversations I've had with people in an attempt to make them feel better about what happened. Unfortunately, while doing so, I lacked empathy in my communication. We seek to "encourage" them by explaining why their feelings are wrong. As Christians, we can be so terrible at this. Check out what Jesus does instead. Jesus wept. Despite knowing Lazarus would be raised from the dead, Jesus pushed past His feelings and mirrored the emotions of those around Him. He empathized with them.

Here's why this display of empathy is even more profound. Let's look back earlier in the chapter in John 11:28-33. In this passage, Jesus requested for Mary to meet Him. When Mary left the house, everyone who mourned with her thought she was going to her brother's tomb and followed her. When she got to the place where Jesus was, she knelt and wept again. Admonishing Him, she cried, "if only you had been here, my brother would not have died" (v. 32, NLT). Jesus saw her weeping and saw the other people who had come with her weeping, and "a deep anger welled up within him, and he was deeply troubled" (v. 33, NLT). Jesus was upset in verse 33, yet He mirrored their weeping in verse 35. I love this because it is a picture of how empathy works. It has nothing to do with how we feel and everything to do with stepping into other people's emotions and feelings. Jesus was troubled by the people's responses. This version says He was angry. However, when He saw their sadness, Jesus wept.

We can have full knowledge and even wisdom on an issue and still respond to others with compassion, servitude, and empathy. Jesus was all-knowing and all-powerful. Yet He was fully human too; and humbled Himself and handled the people who were grieving with care. How can we do the same? How do we respond when people are grieving? Jesus didn't swoop in with "Lift your head!" or quoting Scripture on how they should've been responding. Instead, we see an example of Him prioritizing their

> *His example encourages us to push past our own perspectives and feelings to mirror the disposition of those in front of us as a display of empathy.*

feelings. His example encourages us to push past our own perspectives and feelings to mirror the disposition of those in front of us as a display of empathy. This divine display of compassion in verse 35 humanized Jesus in such a way the people responded in verse 36, "See how much he loved him!" (NLT). Christ's love for Lazarus was evident in the way He empathized with those that were grieving.

I hope this speaks to you as loudly as it spoke to me. That my response to another person's loss is less about knowing the perfect thing to say. It has nothing to do with finding the right words and everything to do with stepping outside of my understanding, knowledge, and even wisdom to experience someone else's feelings and thoughts vicariously. This is how we show our support and love for others. The person in front of us may be in anguish, and we're angry. Yet, how can we push past our emotions and still have an empathetic response?

HOW TO HAVE EMPATHY CONVERSATIONS

According to Merriam-Webster, empathy is "the action of understanding, being aware, being sensitive to, or vicariously experiencing the feelings, thoughts, and experiences of another of either the past or present without having the feelings thoughts and experiences fully communicated in an objectively explicit manner." In short, empathy is about centering others. The idea of vicariously experiencing the thoughts and feelings of another is about our ability to place ourselves in someone else's position and see the situation through their lens. To do this, we need to understand where people are coming from and what they need.

One of the many truths about loss, change, and challenge is that people process it differently. We talked about earlier how grief is highly individualized, and thus our response to it is often different than the person next to us. Even in moments where we're grieving the same loss, we don't necessarily grieve the same way. Again, empathy isn't about us. It's about them. What we think, what we know, and even how we feel takes a back seat to prioritize the person in front of us.

I want to share with you a framework for empathy conversations. This concept came to me as I thought of what this looks like as someone is having a conversation. We talked about how to approach these kinds of conversations to connect by getting A CLUE. Now, let's dive into what this can look like in practice during the conversation.

Empathy Conversations will help you practice how to center the other person as the purpose of emotionally charged conversations. Empathy Conversations is a guide you can use when communicating about change, transition, or loss. Frequently, when it comes to these kinds of conversations, we lead with our conclusions. We start with what we believe, what we think, and how we feel. However, our purpose for the discussion is to connect and understand the perspective and feelings of who we're speaking with.

> *Empathy Conversations will help you practice how to center the other person as the purpose of emotionally charged conversations.*

Generally, when we have a challenging conversation, we are taught to use "I statements." These statements are just as they sound. They may start with "I think/feel..." as a way to express one's perspective without blaming the other person as the cause. These kinds of statements eventually help us gain more clarity on our objective in the conversation and ensure we're discussing actions instead of accusing people of being wrong or bad. While these practices are helpful, I want us to consider an additional way to approach conversations about change, challenge, and loss. I statements begin the conversation by prioritizing our perceptions and our own needs. Before the conversation even happens, we're centering ourselves instead of the other person when we take this approach.

We've repeated empathy isn't about us; it's about centering others—our teammate, friend, family member, colleague, etc. Despite this, our most used approach to hard conversations center our thinking as the initial point of discussion. Instead, Empathy Conversations prioritize the other person over the problem, connection over circumstances, and identity over the issue. Empathy Conversations are used when communicating about change, transition, or loss. There are five priorities of Empathy Conversations: clarify, context, connection, call to action, and commitment. Let's go through each one below and tie in an example of how this works.

Let's imagine you have a colleague, Taylor, who has been laid off from work. You haven't spoken to her yet because you don't know what to say. Let's walk through how to take an **EMPATHY CONVERSATIONS** approach to the dialogue:

EMPATHY CONVERSATIONS

01. CLARIFY

02. CONTEXT

03. CONNECTION

04. CALL TO ACTION

05. COMMITMENT

1. **CLARIFY** *How is the person feeling? What is the person thinking?*

Our Empathy Conversations start with inquiry. Instead of approaching the discussion with our core objective, let's focus on our core question. Since our focus is on the person, we want to ask questions to understand where the person is, his or her feelings, and the person's thinking. Before we can put ourselves in someone else's shoes, we must first understand the mindset of how this person is dealing with this change or loss. Do you have a sense of what he or she is thinking about this loss? Do you know what is top-of-mind and essential? Or are you assuming you do? Are the person's needs met? What gaps may be present? By asking questions, we understand what is top of mind for them.

> *Before we can put ourselves in someone else's shoes, we must first understand the mindset of how this person is dealing with this change or loss.*

Your conversation with Taylor may start with "Hey, Taylor! I was just thinking of you." Followed by a question such as:

- How are you processing all of this?
- What are you most concerned about right now?
- How are you feeling today?
- What questions keep coming to mind that you're working through?

- What do you need most right now?
- What aspect of this experience still raises questions for you?
- What are your thoughts on your next step?

Beginning the conversation with inquiry to gain clarity on how the other person is feeling and thinking will lead you into the next core component of Empathy Conversations—understanding the context of the person's everyday experience.

2. **CONTEXT** *What else is being impacted? How does his or her identity impact the experience?*

In any circumstance involving change, challenge, or loss, external and internal factors are usually impacted by this new outcome. Are you aware of the full context with which the other person has to navigate? In your conversation with Taylor, you may ask yourself questions to better understand her context, such as:

- Are there barriers in the way of your next step?
- Who else in your life are you concerned about since this has happened?
- What priorities do you have now that may have been important but not as urgent before?
- What resources do you need that you can't currently access?
- What else will change as a result of this loss?

Taylor is a seasoned career professional who has worked at the same company for twelve years. Perhaps part of the context surrounding the job loss is that she is the breadwinner for her family. She also has anxiety about updating her resume and creating a LinkedIn profile since she's worked at the same company for so long and hasn't had to do this.

Now, if you had launched into the conversation looking to be a problem solver, sharing all of the details and updates on how to look for jobs via LinkedIn, you likely would have increased Taylor's anxiety around this challenge connected to her loss. However, because you sought to understand the full context of Taylor's loss, you're now set up to make a connection that centers her needs, thoughts, and emotions.

Before we discuss connection, it's essential to recognize the role identity plays in understanding the context. Throughout our dialogue on Taylor, one aspect we haven't addressed is demographics. In what way is Taylor's experience different if Taylor is a white man or a Black woman? What role does gender identity play on job loss experience? If Taylor is a cis-gender wife and mother, how does this impact her experience? The context of our experience is often initially influenced by our identity. Thus, it's critical to keep an open mind to understand the full scope of how the loss is impacting the person in front of you without assumptions.

> *The context of our experience is often initially influenced by our identity.*

3. **CONNECTION** *How can you be what the person needs?*

The three priorities ahead of this one all lead us to the core focus of Empathy Conversations—creating a connection with the other person. Notice how we don't start out trying to be what the person needs. This is important because starting with what you can do to help someone you don't fully understand isn't empathy, it's often performative sympathy that is rooted in helping ourselves feel better about being part of a solution. Until you do the due diligence of clarifying where the person is and understanding the context, you're seeking a connection in the dark. As you better understand where the person is, how they're processing their current circumstances, and the potential outcomes relative to internal or external factors, you are now more aware of potential gaps you could help fill. In your conversation with Taylor, you may say," Thank you for sharing your concerns about your job search process and the impact of LinkedIn and technology in finding your next role. LinkedIn is very comprehensive and can be challenging to learn initially. What would be most helpful for you to know to better navigate the platform?" Because you took the time to clarify, listen, and understand Taylor, you're now connecting in a meaningful way. You are also set up to take an action that supports what Taylor actually needs.

> *Starting with what you can do to help someone you don't fully understand isn't empathy, it's often performative sympathy that is rooted in helping ourselves feel better about being part of a solution.*

4. **CALL TO ACTION** *What support would be helpful for this?*

    Based on how the conversation progresses, you now have an obvious action to take that you know helps Taylor. You could share with her that, "I'd be happy to connect you with a LinkedIn expert I used to help me set up my profile. His name is Landon, and he was excellent to work with and even coached me on how to use some of the job search functionality after setting up my profile. Would you like me to make an email introduction between you two?" As you're connecting, you may uncover additional ways to support her. What other information would be useful for Taylor to know? How will you continue to support her in moving forward? What agreement was made on actions to take for both parties as you move forward? At times, when it comes to hard conversations, this is where we start. We set an objective for the conversation, usually from our own perspective. Then proceed with our "I statement," expressing what we need or want to have happen. While helpful in some circumstances, this can be quite counterproductive for emotionally charged conversations. Empathy Conversations are not about us. They're not about what we think or even how we feel. Instead, our focus is on how we navigate communication to better understand and connect with other people's thoughts, beliefs, and feelings. This helps us with being aware and appreciative of the differences in other people. It also helps us take action that aligns with their needs and not our assumptions. Our call to action comes through connection with the other person, where what's needed to move forward isn't determined by us, but it is revealed through these empathy conversations. Now that we know what action to take, we can look to sustain our support for the other person beyond the conversation.

> *Our call to action comes through connection with the other person, where what's needed to move forward isn't determined by us, but it is revealed through these empathy conversations.*

5. **COMMITMENT** *How will I plan to support the person beyond the present?*

Once we have initiated this conversation with Taylor in mind, we:

- Clarify her feelings and mindset.
- Understand the context of this loss for her.
- Make a real connection centered around Taylor's needs.
- Align on a clear call to action
- And now commit to continued support.

    Empathy Conversations help us connect more deeply. They lead us to a commitment to see the action through and follow up to sustain the other person's objective. For example, you could wrap up your conversation with Taylor by making a mutual commitment to check in with each other in a couple of weeks to see how the LinkedIn profile and resume updates are going. Since you have centered this hard conversation on Taylor's thoughts and needs, it is much more likely the commitment to the next steps and actions moving forward will be sustained. The commitment may sound like a tall order in communication. But I believe this is what leaders sign up for. As a leader, I want to ensure my people know my actions to support them aren't fleeting or all talk without the walk. A commitment means I plan to take action in the future. Beyond the present Empathy Conversation, I live out my words through the action I take beyond the moment.

> *As a leader, I want to ensure my people know my actions to support them aren't fleeting or all talk without the walk. A commitment means I plan to take action in the future.*

As we communicate with others, from business to family and friends, I hope this guide through Empathy Conversations will help you center others in conversations around loss.

THE ORIGINATOR OF EMPATHY CONVERSATIONS

Of the many lessons we learn from the life of Jesus Christ is how He communicated with people. There are three core components to the way He communicated:

AUTHENTIC – His priority of servitude was evident in the way he connected with people authentically.

ATTENTIVE – Focused on the needs, nuance, and knowledge of the people. He mirrored their needs. However he needed to communicate (stories) to reach them, he did it.

ASKED QUESTIONS – His questions helped people gain a deeper understanding of themselves and connection with Him.

One of my favorite lessons on having uncomfortable conversations is found in the story of Jesus and the Samaritan Woman. While there are many commentaries and sermons about this story in John 4, I believe one of the most powerful lessons to be learned is how Jesus communicated with the Samaritan woman.

When I read this story, I am so struck by His cadence, tone, and choice of words in their dialogue. Let's walk through the story in John Chapter 4 together:

THE WOMAN AT THE WELL (MSG)

__4 1-3__ Jesus realized that the Pharisees were keeping count of the baptisms that he and John performed (although his disciples, not Jesus, did the actual baptizing). They had posted the score that Jesus was ahead, turning him and John into rivals in the eyes of the people. So Jesus left the Judean countryside and went back to Galilee.

__4-6__ To get there, he had to pass through Samaria. He came into Sychar, a Samaritan village that bordered the field Jacob had given his son Joseph. Jacob's well was still there. Jesus, worn out by the trip, sat down at the well. It was noon.

__7-8__ A woman, a Samaritan, came to draw water. Jesus said, "Would you give me a drink of water?" (His disciples had gone to the village to buy food for lunch.)
__9__ The Samaritan woman, taken aback, asked, "How come you, a Jew, are asking me, a Samaritan woman, for a drink?" (Jews in those days wouldn't be caught dead talking to Samaritans.)

10 Jesus answered, "If you knew the generosity of God and who I am, you would be asking me for a drink, and I would give you fresh, living water."

11-12 The woman said, "Sir, you don't even have a bucket to draw with, and this well is deep. So how are you going to get this 'living water'? Are you a better man than our ancestor Jacob, who dug this well and drank from it, he and his sons and livestock, and passed it down to us?"

13-14 Jesus said, "Everyone who drinks this water will get thirsty again and again. Anyone who drinks the water I give will never thirst—not ever. The water I give will be an artesian spring within, gushing fountains of endless life."

15 The woman said, "Sir, give me this water so I won't ever get thirsty, won't ever have to come back to this well again!"

16 He said, "Go call your husband and then come back."

17-18 "I have no husband," she said.
"That's nicely put: 'I have no husband.' You've had five husbands, and the man you're living with now isn't even your husband. You spoke the truth there, sure enough."

19-20 "Oh, so you're a prophet! Well, tell me this: Our ancestors worshiped God at this mountain, but you Jews insist that Jerusalem is the only place for worship, right?"

21-23 "Believe me, woman, the time is coming when you Samaritans will worship the Father neither here at this mountain nor there in Jerusalem.

You worship guessing in the dark; we Jews worship in the clear light of day. God's way of salvation is made available through the Jews. But the time is coming—it has come—when what you're called will not matter and where you go to worship will not matter.

23-24 *"It's who you are and the way you live that count before God. Your worship must engage your spirit in the pursuit of truth. That's the kind of people the Father is out looking for: those who are simply and honestly themselves before him in their worship. God is sheer being itself—Spirit. Those who worship him must do it out of their very being, their spirits, their true selves, in adoration."*

25 *The woman said, "I don't know about that. I do know that the Messiah is coming. When he arrives, we'll get the whole story."*
26 *"I am he," said Jesus. "You don't have to wait any longer or look any further."*

27 *Just then his disciples came back. They were shocked. They couldn't believe he was talking with that kind of a woman. No one said what they were all thinking, but their faces showed it.*

28-30 *The woman took the hint and left. In her confusion, she left her water pot. Back in the village, she told the people, "Come see a man who knew all about the things I did, who knows me inside and out. Do you think this could be the Messiah?" And they went out to see for themselves.*

39-42 Many of the Samaritans from that village committed themselves to him because of the woman's witness: "He knew all about the things I did. He knows me inside and out!" They asked him to stay on, so Jesus stayed two days. A lot more people entrusted their lives to him when they heard what he had to say. They said to the woman, "We're no longer taking this on your say-so. We've heard it for ourselves and know it for sure. He's the Savior of the world!"

Now maybe you're familiar with this story, or perhaps you just read it for the first time. Either way, I want to share with you this incredible model of how to have uncomfortable conversations:

- The first thing we notice is how Jesus started the conversation with the woman—by asking a question. This is powerful because I don't think He would've had any problem getting the water for Himself. But I believe this expresses how starting with inquiry is genuinely the way to connect in conversation. It represents our interdependence on one another and gives us an opportunity for better emotional intelligence. We see in this example, Jesus asked her for something He could have provided for Himself.

- She responded by acknowledging their differences. She's like, listen, you're a Jew, and I'm a Samaritan woman. Why are you asking me for a drink when we're not even supposed to be associating at all? Keep this in mind. We will come back to the cultural differences she believed would keep them from communicating effectively, as this is so relevant today.

- Jesus' response recognized her frame of reference—noting if she knew the identity of the One who asked for the drink, she would be the one asking questions. He started with an inquiry to tap into her feelings and mindset.

- Then we see this shift in the conversation. Jesus seeks to understand her and discuss her context. He mentions her husband, to which she responds she doesn't have a husband. This shift in the conversation signals how Jesus not only cared about her current circumstances, but He also cared about her context and condition.

- This created an opportunity for Jesus to connect with the Samaritan woman. Until this point, we notice she's perplexed by the conversation. But I would say it's this shift that pulls her in. This connection is necessary. We see it often in how Jesus communicated and influenced others to action. It's easy to skip over this connection part in communication with other people because we're so focused on what we want to share, how we feel, and what we want the other person to know. However, it's crucial to understand how people think and the context of their experience to create a genuine connection and call to action.

- We see in verses 19–20; she recognized Jesus as a prophet. I believe this connection built a trust level replacing her confusion and allowing her to be receptive to what Jesus shared next in verses 21–24. As we're thinking about conversations in our own lives, how do we model connection that replaces confusion in communication and builds trust?

> *It's crucial to understand how people think and the context of their experience to create a genuine connection and call to action.*

- In verse 21, Jesus prophesized about the day the Samaritans would worship the Father and the pathway for salvation. The way Jesus communicated with the woman is so powerful that verse 28 says this woman—who came to this well to draw water—is so transformed she leaves the very thing she came for (the water and water jar) and returns with so much more!

- Remember how the woman referred to Jesus as different from her and how this meant they shouldn't be speaking? Jesus' connection with this woman is so powerful. Check out how she references Him in verse 29—not as a Jew or someone else. She exclaimed to her, homegirls, "Come, see a man." This is the same woman who in verse 9, in response to Jesus asking for water, made a comment about His audacity to speak to her based on His identity and cultural difference. By the end of the empathetic encounter, she doesn't refer to Jesus through the lens of their differences, but she humanizes Him as a man everyone should meet. Powerful.

- This interaction is so powerful for her that she returns and brings other people to experience the transformation she just had. She helped to influence the belief of many other Samaritans through her testimony. They also became believers. Rather than continuing on His journey, Jesus stayed there with them for two additional days (see v. 40).

How do we communicate like Jesus? If you think about the full context of this story, there was nothing at the end of the story that Jesus wasn't aware of initially. However, He didn't begin the conversation pointing out her sins, "Here you come with all your husbands." He didn't start the conversation with His objective (her salvation), His title, or a series of "I statements." She didn't recognize who He was, yet His focus was on her the entire time. Look at the themes we have here: compassion for others; genuine curiosity to understand the people we're talking to; concern about their context and condition; connecting in a personable way before influencing their action. This is the communication model Jesus Christ shows us in this powerful story and throughout Scripture.

How often do we model this flow of communication? Do we start with clarifying where people are to understand how they're thinking about the topic of conversation before we dive headfirst into our agenda? This can be a make-or-break in hard, emotionally-charged discussions with colleagues, family members, or friends.

One of my favorite quotes on leadership is how great leaders cultivate more leaders. As a leader, I want to empower my team to elevate their capacity to lead and grow beyond where they are. Aiding in their development in this way requires a level of intentionality in our communication. As we lead others to engage in communication through empathy and connection, we help the team to gain a deeper understanding of their own capacity and capability to lead. How are you communicating with those around you? The goal isn't to know what to say in every situation. But rather, as leaders, it's to shift our focus to understanding and creating space to discuss others' mindset and feelings. This includes caring enough about their context to make a real connection before we share what it is that we think we know. I can't tell you how much I appreciated empathy conversations in the early months of my grief journey, and those connections have been critical to helping me deal, heal, and thrive through it.

> *As we lead others to engage in communication through empathy and connection, we help the team to gain a deeper understanding of their own capacity and capability to lead.*

Thoughts along the journey:

5. Have the Tough Conversations

What conversations have you been putting off because they're uncomfortable?

What makes these conversations uncomfortable?

List who you need to have these conversations with and think of the core question you want to ask to facilitate an Empathy Conversation?

What is the next step you will take to have one of these conversations within the next month?

SECTION THREE
GRACE

"I will hold myself to a standard of grace, not perfection."

– UNKNOWN

CHAPTER 6

Managing Your Mindset

"When we are no longer able to change a situation, we are challenged to change ourselves."
– DR. VIKTOR FRANKL

As we think through having these tough conversations and asking meaningful questions, it's vital to consider how we manage our mindset. We talk about managing our emotions when perhaps the real challenge is managing how we filter our thoughts. The word manage means to direct, be in charge of, or handle a degree of skill. When we manage a project, we actively engage in directing activities related to achieving the desired outcome from start to finish. When we take on a title as a manager, we accept the responsibility to initiate engagement with a cross-functional team to develop and reach the desired goal. There is a sense of responsibility and accountability to the people or projects we've been entrusted in both of these examples. We can relate to the sense of duty and daily responsibility for these tasks. However, sometimes, when it comes to managing our mindset, we don't account for the day-to-day engagement and commitment to direct and be in charge of our thoughts. Have you ever considered what it means to have a sound mind?

If you look up having a sound mind, you may find some medical definitions dealing with having the capacity to think, understand, and reason. When we're experiencing change, challenge, and loss, the ability to think, understand, and reflect on our thinking can be disrupted. How often do you assess your thoughts? In this chapter, we will review the importance of taking our thoughts captive to manage our mindset. But first, let's talk about why this can be so challenging in the first place.

THE TENSION BETWEEN WHAT YOU KNOW AND HOW YOU FEEL

One of the most challenging aspects of resilience is the tension between what we know and how we feel. Normally, it isn't until we're going through some kind of change, challenge, or loss that our mental fortitude is tested. This is because, before these crossroad moments, there is often a seamless synergy between what we know, what we're experiencing, and how we feel. When disruption shows up, that synergy starts to feel more like psychotic chaos. That isn't an observation I've made of others or an idea I've researched. I'm sharing what I've experienced.

> *One of the most challenging aspects of resilience is the tension between what we know and how we feel.*

I vividly remember being pulled down the hallway of Summit Hospital's Intensive Care Unit by my brothers just after 5 p.m. CDT on June 5, 2017. As soon as I stepped around the corner into the room, past family members, and saw my mother's lifeless body lying on the bed, it felt like my head was going to explode. I have never experienced that kind of physical pain in my life! It's hard to even adequately describe it in words. Yes, I was crying. My heart was shattered, and I had this excruciating pain in my head. I was so undone emotionally that I even became physically sick and vomited. In the days following, I had moments where I felt as if I was losing my mind. I was trying to reconcile the fact that my mother wasn't coming around the corner to sit at the kitchen table to ask how New York was or agree to let me play kitchen cosmetologist to wash and color her hair. In the midst of this, I was utterly shocked and at a loss for words even still to describe the grief and guilt of not being there when she took her last breath. I was busy working hard and proving I was the right woman for the job, who couldn't ask for time off to be with my mom just yet because I was trying to prove I was a hard worker by my willingness (and visibility) to be in the office past 5pm. I was trying to calculate when to ask and how to ask and what it may mean. All the while, my mother was dying while I was trying to prove I belonged. You see, I know Christ. I believe He makes no mistakes. I trusted He would heal her. Yet, He took her minutes before I arrived? Minutes.

The fluctuation between how I felt and what I knew felt like being on a roller coaster ride that was never going to end. Despite grappling with the guilt connected to my grief, there was still a job to do in these early days—one final act involving my mother. Our brains are so powerful because even during these moments of deep pain, we can still will our way through tasks that must get done. We needed to plan a legacy celebration—with excellence, intention, and thoughtful regard. During these early times of grief, I knew what needed to get done despite how I was feeling. I had to channel my feelings to execute what needed to get done.

In moments like this, we must be aware of and intentional in how we respond to the differences between what we know and how we feel. Specifically, it becomes critical to filter how we feel through the lens of what we know when the two compete with one another. The fluctuation of emotion in moments of change, challenge, loss, and trauma can be devastating. We feel things emotionally and physically; we've never felt before. We feel pain in new and seemingly unbearable ways. In times like this, it becomes critical to develop a practice of bringing our feelings under the submission of what we know. Now, this doesn't mean you don't feel your feelings, or you ignore them. The first rest stop on this resilience roadmap is to acknowledge how we feel. It is so critically important we do this because our instinct—particularly type A, ambitious people—can be to bulldoze straight through our feelings. We know they're there. But we don't have time to deal with them. However, if this is our norm or way of protecting ourselves, we're committing on this journey to take a different route. We want to acknowledge the feelings we have and remind ourselves of what we know. This helps us to reframe and eventually reimagine as we process our emotions.

Now let me say this doesn't happen on its own. Most of us will find ourselves towards the end of one side of the spectrum— flowing with every feeling we have or pretending we don't feel anything as we "get over it." Let's talk about how we manage our mindset and the tension between feeling and knowing. When we're going through situations, leaving us emotional and overwhelmed, we must be grounded in what we know by recalling the truths we live by. This is the work. The moments that challenge us the deepest will reveal what we believe. What are the principles of truth which guide your life?

When I say the truth, I mean the absolute foundational principles in your life that remain the same regardless of the changes around you. For me, those principles are grounded in the Christian faith. The word of God is my center of Truth. I believe Jesus Christ is the way, the truth, and the life. Because this is my guiding belief, this truth becomes the filter through which I funnel my feelings. Your truth—your guiding belief grounding the life you live—becomes the mirror by which you manage your mindset. This is powerful because often, we find ourselves in moments of loss looking outside of ourselves for something (sometimes anything) to grab on to so we can just survive. I want to encourage you that you can survive the loss, the tragedy, the change, the challenge, and even the trauma. Through your mental awareness, grit, and grace, you can thrive through this.

> *When we're going through situations, leaving us emotional and overwhelmed, we must be grounded in what we know by recalling the truths we live by. This is the work.*

> *Your truth – your guiding belief grounding the life you live – becomes the mirror by which you manage your mindset.*

What is the foundation for truth in your life? How do you determine your reference for understanding those things beyond you? Where do you look to remind yourself of what you know? Having a sound mind, despite our capacity to know why something is happening, is tied to how we process what we know. This helps us balance the uncertainty. A simple exercise to put this into practice is taking out a sheet of paper or pulling up the notes section of your phone or a Word document on your device and writing down what you know. I did this on the car ride, on my way to my mother's funeral.

My brothers and I agreed we would speak at mom's funeral. When my sweet husband was creating the program for her service, we didn't know who exactly would speak or if one of us would speak for all of us. I asked Joe to type in "Tribute to Our Mother" and list all of our names. In the days leading up to her service, it was hard to believe I was preparing to speak at my mom's funeral. What? How? I wanted to prepare something to say, but the words never came when I tried to think about it. In the car, with my brothers, sisters-in- love, nieces, nephew, husband, and dad, I pulled out my phone. Here's what I wrote (still in my notes):

Feelings and Knowledge

Easter at 4/5 yrs old - her knowing, my feelings

WHAT I KNOW:

1. Daddy: Romans 8:18 Look to the joy that was and is and is to come.

2. Brothers, family & friends: John 15:5 her fruit... Bryan and Troy - strong family men, Christian men, priests, providers, and protectors of their home. She was proud of that. And all of her many children ... extended family & friends. I see her fruit in you, in all the memories that have been shared this week. And her friends that were there to the very

end, even when I couldn't be. You know who you are, and I appreciate you more than you know. Thank you.

3. Her lessons on love: Luke 10:27 And he answered, "You shall love the Lord your God with all your heart and with all your soul and with all your strength and with all your mind, and your neighbor as yourself."

I walked up to the podium last after both of my brothers had spoken so beautifully. Still, with the notes above on my phone, I wasn't sure what would come out. It was almost like a complete out of body experience. I'm standing there behind a closed casket, preparing to share about my mother in the past tense. It was a surreal moment. As I was still gathering my thoughts, I started singing "Grateful" by Hezekiah Walker. Then it came to me: "Share what you know." I started telling a story of how my mother always encouraged me to embrace discomfort and speak regardless of how I feel. I shared Romans 8:18 and talked about the struggle between what we feel and what we know and tried to encourage my family and myself how everything we were feeling at that moment was the opposite of the outcome we wanted. Despite the feeling, in order not to be overcome by it, we must remind ourselves of what we know. This was the only thing helping me through many moments—constant reflection and repeating the foundational, immutable truths in my life.

Romans 8:18 has been a grounding foundational truth in my life to help reconcile my present pain with a future promise. It says, "For I consider that the sufferings of this present time are not worth comparing with the glory that is to be revealed to us" (ESV). This foundational truth helps me have the capacity to think beyond how I'm feeling and rest on hope in the future I cannot presently see but know exists. What is your foundational truth? What is it you know needs to be prioritized over the way you feel? Maybe it isn't a Scripture reference. Perhaps you need to know you are enough—beautifully and wonderfully made. You are royalty. You are precious. You have within you everything you need to be and do what it is you were destined to become. I believe this practice of reminding ourselves of what we know is what it means when Paul talks about God's strength being made perfect in our weakness. We can feel weak, and God still strengthens our mind, heart, spirit, and soul.

In the space below, list three of your foundational truths. What do you know?

_____
_____
_____
_____
_____
_____
_____
_____
_____
_____
_____
_____
_____
_____
_____

TAKING YOUR THOUGHTS CAPTIVE

Let's recap this critical step in managing our mindset. How do you develop your mindset? One practice is to be aware of and assess your thoughts or to take your thoughts captive. When we are more aware of what we think, we can start to make shifts in how we think. Being aware of your thoughts is such a critical part of maintaining a sound mind. We often don't even recognize the negative self-talk and self-sabotage thinking we allow to permeate our mind and then flow from our mouth. It's not that we won't have negative thoughts. We will. Even as we grow and develop, we still must manage our mindset, so we aren't ruled by doubt, fear, and untruths at the new level we've reached. The goal is to manage how we think by taking our thoughts **C.A.P.T.I.V.E.** Hopefully, by now, you've come to love acronyms and acrostics, too!

Let's recap how we take our thoughts captive:

CHALLENGE – When you have an unwanted thought entering your mind, challenge it. You challenge your thoughts by interrupting them and asking yourself, "Why do I think that?"

AWARENESS – As you make challenging your thoughts a habit, it will raise your awareness of how you think. How often do you pause to think about how you think? As you acknowledge your thoughts, you will become more aware of what triggers certain thoughts or feelings.

PERSIST – Shifting your energy to move past the thought requires fortitude. As you consistently raise your awareness by challenging your thoughts, you will begin to set a filter for the thoughts you dismiss, decide to push past, or replace.

TRUTH – When you have a thought that doesn't serve you, it's not enough to dismiss it. Typically, when we do this, the idea will re-emerge. It's important to replace negative thoughts with the truth. Affirmations and Bible verses are excellent sources of truth for replacing negative thoughts. To ensure you have resources available for this, check out the #thrivethroughit affirmations I developed at brittanyncole.com.

INTENTION – As powerful as our minds are, they don't necessarily renew on their own. To take your thoughts captive, set an intention for where you will focus.

VISION – Our vision guides our intention for our thoughts. Do you see yourself the way you want to be? Are you setting your vision as a north star? Create a vision for your life that guides your intention. Who do you want to become? What impact do you want to have? What is your next best move?

EVERY DAY – The secret is there is no secret. To master your mindset, you will repeat these strategies daily until they are habits for how you guard your thoughts. We don't get to do these steps once and then think we've conquered negative thoughts forever. This is an everyday practice.

As you deal with a problematic colleague or push past imposter syndrome, or grieve the loss of a loved one, taking your thoughts **CAPTIVE** will help you manage your mindset as you give yourself grace in this new space.

PERSONAL THOUGHT LEADERSHIP & AFFIRMATIONS TO MANAGE YOUR MINDSET

As leaders, personal development becomes more critical as we grow and advance our careers and teams. I live by the motto that every experience is an opportunity for continuous improvement. That means the good experiences and especially the bad ones. Because I believe this to be true, I cannot run away from difficult moments, difficult conversations, or difficult people.

I can remember my first promotion with relocation. It was the third time I applied for this role, and this particular position would take me to a city I never thought I'd live in—Chattanooga, TN. Before relocating from Nashville to Chattanooga, I'd built some rapport with my new team through the interview process. Everyone was so pleasant, kind, and helpful except for one teammate. She made it very clear when I reached out before my first interview that she had also applied for the role, was currently doing the work, and didn't have much to share with me. After I hung up from our call, I made a note not to call her back unless I got the job, in which case she would be my partner. I got the job.

My first time meeting the team in person was at a holiday dinner party in December. I walked into the restaurant's private dining room, met my new team and their spouses, and my new partner walked past me without speaking. For the next four years, our working relationship went from toxic to transformational. There are many stories I could share here, but they all have one thing in common. I had to decide to see the situation differently and choose how to engage with my partner. Now I'm in no way advocating for staying in toxic environments. However, part of thriving through is managing our mindset around what we're experiencing when we have difficulty. My colleague went from not acknowledging my presence to asking me to coach her through an interview, to inviting me to her daughter's wedding. I worked with her in many challenging moments. But I'm so grateful for our encounters and the lessons I learned to manage my mindset through a hard-working relationship. How do you remind yourself of the truth of what you know despite being in the midst of loss?

Here are some affirmations to help you manage your mindset (For the complete deck of affirmations, visit brittanyncole.com/shop.):

AFFIRMATIONS TO MANAGE YOUR MINDSET

I am more than enough and absolutely capable of leading projects and people. Leadership is a skill I have and continue to develop consistently.

I value a productive blend of work and life priorities every day. I will be aware of how I can effectively and efficiently prioritize my day. If everything is important, nothing is important.

I am responsible for my happiness and career development. I will initiate the necessary conversations to thrive in the workplace.

I am supposed to be right where I am. My brilliance, training, and experiences have gotten me where I am. I'm also grateful for having the assistance of others who support me. I will not shrink.

What's happening to me doesn't define me. I will acknowledge my feelings while also taking my thoughts captive to thrive through it.

I believe I can, and I will. All things are possible as long as I continue to believe. Half of doing is believing. I am building what I first believe.

Today I will decide to see all the good around me—even if I have to squint. I am right where I'm meant to be and will learn something new today.

Every experience is an opportunity for continuous improvement. I'm prepared and ready to learn, grow, and improve.

I am creating the ideal work experience I want and enjoying the lessons along the way. Every circumstance I find myself in today will work out for my good.

I thrive under pressure and also know how to use my voice and boundaries to prevent burnout. If I need help, I will ask. If I'm uncomfortable, I will speak up. I am motivated and have everything I need to thrive through any obstacle.

I am open-minded and always looking to learn from every experience. I continuously push myself to develop in areas that stretch my skill set and bring me happiness, freedom, and purpose.

I am becoming. I will hold myself to challenging but realistic expectations of what I can achieve today. I will celebrate each goal I accomplish with gratitude and joy. Every

> *decision I make brings me closer to my goal and the best version of myself.*
>
> *I am resilient. Resilience isn't about my ability to bounce back. It's also about being brave enough to be honest, and transparent with someone else about where I've been, where I am, and where I'm going. Today I will share my story with someone else to encourage them to keep thriving!*

REIMAGINE, REASSESS, AND REINVENT

Resilience is a skill and one that you may not realize the depth of your capacity until after you've experienced a loss. It requires us to accept our new reality, have challenging conversations, and discover purpose in our new and next normal. One way to make the present reality—the change, challenge, or loss—manageable is to find meaning through it. Viktor E. Frankl, an Austrian neurologist, psychiatrist, and Auschwitz concentration camp survivor, wrote a book called Man's Search for Meaning, where he described a pivotal moment in the camp, now known as meaning therapy.

> *Resilience is a skill and one that you may not realize the depth of your capacity until after you've experienced a loss.*

In his book, he shares how he was on his way to work at the concentration camp one day, worrying about how to work with a new foreman whom he knew to be particularly sadistic. He was disgusted by how trivial and meaningless his life had become but realized he had to find some purpose to survive. Frankl did so by imagining himself beyond his present reality. He imagined himself giving a lecture after the war on the psychology of concentration camps to help outsiders understand what he had been through. Although unsure how he would survive, Frankl created some concrete goals for himself. In doing so, he succeeded in rising above the sufferings of the moment. As he shares in his book, we must remember to find meaning when we're met with seemingly hopeless situations that we can't change.[11]

Are you finding meaning in your present challenge by reimaging who you will become? To reimagine means to imagine anew. One of the core components of reimagining your future is recognizing your current situation isn't only about you. The story of your present challenge could be the key to unlock a door for someone else. You will notice how Dr. Frankl reimagined himself thriving through his unimaginable daily experiences to share his story to help others. His story, research, and training (www.viktorfrankl.org/) is now a standard of practice assisting organizations worldwide. This is where resilience starts—in our mind, with a vision of how we see ourselves on the other side of our present pain. Now I'd be remiss if I didn't share that Dr. Frankl isn't the first to coin this concept. One of my favorite passages of Scripture is in Hebrews 12:2, a section that is all about endurance, discipline, and resilience. Verse 2 says this, "looking to Jesus, the founder and perfecter of our faith, who for the joy that was set before him endured the cross, despising the shame, and is seated at the right hand of the throne of God" (ESV). Some like to jump to the end, the triumphant position of being seated in a place of influence. But did you catch the purpose-filled

---

[11] Frankl, Viktor E. (Viktor Emil), 1905-1997. Man's Search for Meaning; an Introduction to Logotherapy. Boston :Beacon Press, 1962.

perspective it took to get there? For the JOY that was set before Jesus, He endured the cross. Christ endured the cross because He focused on the vision in front of Him. The purpose behind the pain of the cross and the vision of what would come through it helped Him endure. What vision of joy do you have beyond your present pain?

The beauty of loss is that it helps us reprioritize what matters most in our lives. When we experience profound loss, we're challenged to reflect on the parts of our lives we're often too busy to spend reflective time on. Often deep loss changes us. We begin to reassess our priorities and practices and measure them against the clearer vision we have of who we want to become and how we want to impact others. This self-reflection journey and re-discovery may cause us to reinvent, to reflect our new desires, boundaries, and priorities. We will talk about ways to reinvent yourself later in Chapter 9. For now, let's look at how you can reimagine your life to reinvent.

> *The beauty of loss is that it helps us reprioritize what matters most in our lives.*

A MODEL FOR REIMAGINING

Managing our mindset through loss helps us get to a place where we can reimagine a new way forward. As we journey through—not over, around, or looking backward—our mindset determines our ability to reimagine so we can reinvent. How do we reimagine? I believe our ability to reimagine amid change, challenge, and loss depends on four areas we must assess and identify: our beliefs, values, vision, and decisions.

Managing our mindset through loss helps us get to a place where we can reimagine a new way forward. Our ability to reimagine depends on our beliefs, values, vision, and decisions.

Spend some time in introspection and write down your thoughts on this model for reimagining:

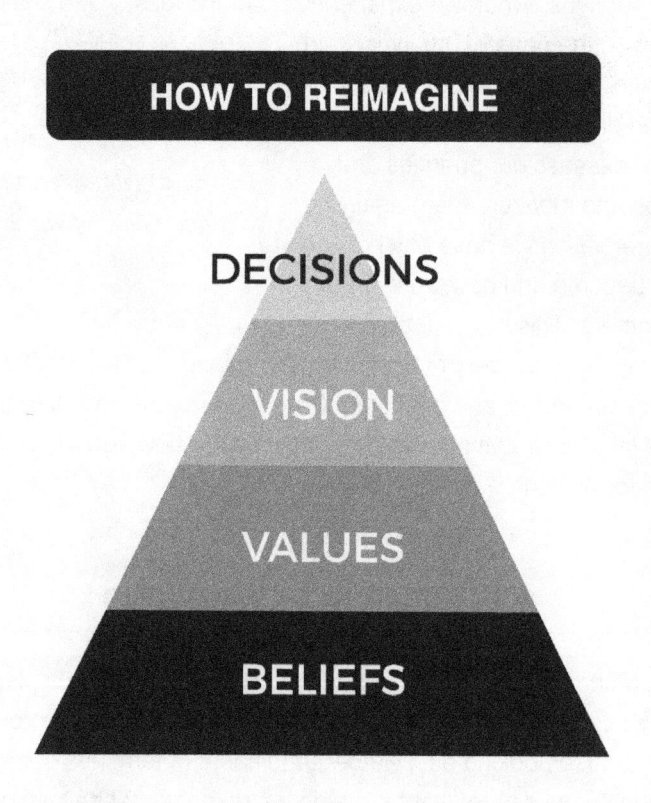

HOW TO REIMAGINE

- DECISIONS
- VISION
- VALUES
- BELIEFS

1. Our beliefs are what ground us. They are the foundation we stand on, especially when journeying through loss. What we believe will be where we place our trust. This enables us to have the fortitude to journey forward even when we can't see every single step. Please understand. I'm not asking you about your religion or spiritual beliefs, necessarily. The question isn't what have you been taught to think. I'm asking, what do you know for sure? What are your core beliefs? What do you believe? We must take the time to do the work to consider in what/whom we've placed our trust. When you think about the present challenge or loss in your life, what are your core beliefs?

Here are some areas to consider to uncover your core beliefs:
- What guides you when you have to make hard decisions?
- What do you believe to be true at this moment?
- When you're at your lowest, who do you turn to?
- What family and childhood lessons have you learned?
- How would you describe your faith?
- What are the top three things you believe in right now?

2. Our values are the principles that frame how we think and act out our beliefs. In essence, our beliefs help us shape our values. Think of your values as guides or your way of being in the world. One of my favorite resources for determining personal values is Brene' Brown's book, Dare to Lead. In it, she describes the importance of contemplating our values so we can name them and live them out. We don't have a set of professional values and a set of personal values. We only have one set of values that guide us in every area and circumstance of our life. Here is a brief list of values below. What are your values?

Here are three questions from Dare to Lead to help you name your values.

ASK YOURSELF:

Does this define me? Is this who I am at my best?
Is this a filter that I use to make hard decisions

Accomplishment	Hard work	Peace
Accountability	Harmony	Power
Achievement	Health	Quality
Balance	Improvement	Reason
Beauty	Innovation	Recognition
Boldness	Integrity	Respect
Challenge	Joy	Responsibility
Connection	Justice	Risk
Creativity	Kindness	Satisfaction
Decisiveness	Knowledge	Self-reliance
Development	Learning	Service
Discovery	Love	Stewardship
Efficiency	Loyalty	Teamwork
Empathy	Meaning	Transparency
Equality	Moderation	Understanding
Family	Motivation	Uniqueness
Fortitude	Openness	Unity
Freedom	Optimism	Vision
Generosity	Order	Wealth
Grace	Patience	Wisdom
Gratitude		

Of course, this is not an exhaustive list. But it will help to get you started. You can find additional resources on determining your personal values at brenebrown.com/daretolead

3. Our Vision is the gateway for reimaging to reinvent. Now that you're clear on your beliefs and values, it's time to see what hasn't been seen. What is the vision you have of where you're headed next? Now you may be thinking, "I had a vision, and this wasn't it." I hear you. That's the hard part about change, challenge, and loss. Life can completely shift the path we thought we'd take towards accomplishing our goals. The key, however, is to know we will always come to a place where we refine our vision. If you wear eyeglasses, you know what this is like. You walk into the optometrist seeing fine. Then you go through the exam and realize there's an opportunity for you to see even better. You leave seeing better than you realized you could before you came. This is what it looks like to refine our vision to reimagine going beyond what we thought we were capable of.

For personal leadership, ask yourself:

- Where am I being led to impact next? What kind of life do I want to live? How do I want to impact the lives of other people? What lessons have I learned from this? What am I being called to do next? What am I doing when I have the most joy? Who do I want to become?

For leading people and teams, here are some tips on crafting a vision to reimagine your future:

- A vision reveals purpose – Renowned author Jim Collins of the business classic Good to Great calls your vision a BHAG "big hairy audacious goal." "A BHAG serves as a unifying focal point of effort, galvanizing people, and creating team spirit as people strive toward a finish line."

- A vision can help you stand out from your competition – Zappos CEO Tony Hsieh differentiated his company from every other internet retailer by casting a vision of Delivering Happiness.

- A vision involves contributions from a wide range of people – According to The Work of Leaders: How Vision, Alignment and Execution Will Change the Way You Lead, leaders at all levels are responsible for crafting a vision. How can you tap into the leaders across your organization to co-create a vision that elevates your work, sparks imagination, and inspires people to do meaningful, values-driven work?

4. Our Decisions are where the rubber meets the road, as they say. The purpose of reimagining is to take action towards your new and next normal. Often when we experience change, challenge, and loss, it can be difficult for us to imagine what feels like a a complete 180 degree change in our lives. Although big changes often feel this way, the way we get to reinvention is through the smaller decisions we choose to make every day. What new decisions do you need to make to become who you need to be to manifest the vision you have for your life? Those daily decisions will determine how your vision manifests in the world.

Thoughts along the journey:

6. Reimagine to Reinvent the Now You

In the space below, list your responses for how you will reimagine to reinvent:

I BELIEVE...

_____
_____
_____
_____
_____
_____
_____
_____
_____
_____
_____
_____
_____
_____

MY VALUES ARE...

_____
_____
_____
_____
_____
_____
_____
_____
_____
_____

MY VISION FOR MY LIFE IS...

_____
_____
_____
_____
_____
_____
_____
_____
_____
_____

THE NEXT DECISIONS I NEED TO MAKE ARE...

CHAPTER 7

Self-Care Is Resilience

"You don't have anything to give that you don't have. So you have to keep your own self full. Fill your cup up. Your real work is to figure out where your power base is and to work on the alignment of your personality and gifts with the real reason why you're here."
– OPRAH WINFREY

"How you treat yourself is how you treat God. You are the representation of God in your life."
– IYANLA VANZANT

These quotes are a reminder of the very familiar phrase in Psalm 23:5, "my cup runneth over" (KJV). As much as I love Oprah, Iyanla, and all of the gurus of self-care, this idea of taking care of ourselves to be of service to other people is a Biblical principle that we often miss. In this passage, David shows us the abundant and overflowing nature of God's presence and provision designed to fill us and then spill over to bless others. It reminds us how the blessings of overflow we receive are meant to be a channel we pour out to others. Essentially, self-care and service go hand-in-hand. Yet, to be strong and prove our strength for many of us, we often skip the self-care part. Think of self-care as your prerequisite for service. If you want to serve more expansively, fill your cup.

> *Think of self-care as your prerequisite for service. If you want to serve more expansively, fill your cup.*

WHY IS SELF-CARE IMPORTANT FOR BUSINESS?

As business leaders, we don't usually spend much time considering the impact of self-care. It feels like more of a personal or lifestyle concern. Let's talk about why this may not be the case. If you're like me, self-care is an area you've had to focus on. I'm a type-A, make it happen, yes we can, exceed expectations, both and leader who can easily slip into all gas and no brakes kind of days. This is especially true in the midst of a crisis or a significant shift.

When we experience change, challenge, and loss, often, the speed of transition is constant and increasing. There is always more to be done and seemingly fewer resources to work with. In situations such as this (or years—hi, 2020), resilience becomes critical. As change is happening at a rapid pace, we must acknowledge, adapt, and adjust constantly. Our ability to effectively navigate these seasons of life and business is connected to our psychological wellbeing. Self-care helps us

> *Self-care helps us prioritize our mental, emotional, and physical wellbeing—which results in us showing up better, more attentive, focused, and productive for other people.*

prioritize our mental, emotional, and physical wellbeing—which results in us showing up better, more attentive, focused, and productive for other people. According to the American Psychological Association Center for Organizational Excellence, a psychologically healthy workplace is one that enhances performance and productivity while fostering their employees' health and well-being across five categories – employee involvement, work-life synergy, employee growth and development, health and safety, and employee recognition. Organizations that meet these criteria of a psychologically healthy workplace benefit from improved work quality and productivity, lower absenteeism, presenteeism, less turnover, and better customer service ratings.[12]

> *Organizations that meet these criteria of a psychologically healthy workplace benefit from improved work quality and productivity, lower absenteeism, presenteeism, less turnover, and better customer service ratings.*

Successful entrepreneurs, corporate executives, non-profit leaders, and business owners know the value of health and wellness. Jeff Bezos, CEO of Amazon, knows the importance of self-care. In 2018, he shared with the Economic Club of Washington, D.C. how he takes time to rest, recharge, and make decisions carefully.

---

[12] Creating a Psychologically Healthy Workplace. American Psychological Association Center for Organizational Excellence.
https://www.apaexcellence.org/resources/creatingahealthyworkplace/

Jeff Bezos shared that he:

- Goes to bed early to wake up early
- Eats breakfast with his family and reads the newspaper to start his workday
- Schedules his first meeting that requires the most brainpower for 10 a.m. (high IQ meetings before lunch)
- Sets a boundary for the end of the day by 5:00 p.m
- Needs eight hours of sleep to think better, have more energy, and be in a better mood.

"Think about it, as a senior executive, what do you really get paid to do?" Bezos says, "As a senior executive, you get paid to make a small number of high-quality decisions." He encourages leaders if you don't take care of yourself, "the quality of those decisions might be lower because you're tired or grouchy or any number of things."

How are you planning out your day to prioritize your self-care? Yes, high performance is essential. Yes, you're likely leading a team or large project the organization is counting on. Or yes, you're the CEO. Your company's success is connected to your leadership. Either or all of those may be true for you. It's essential to understand the cost of not taking care of yourself and how this could mean more than the investment of creating boundaries to be your best self. Burnout is a slippery slope that is very real for far too many leaders.

Your company's success is connected to your leadership.

Simply put, we can't lead others well if we aren't taking care of ourselves. This is why self-care is so critical. One of the primary reasons we often put self-care on the back burner is to wear a badge of honor for how hard we work. Listen, overwork, and overwhelm is not a sign of value or badge of honor. Having a lack of self-care as a leader sets a counterproductive precedent for your team. As a Black woman in corporate America, I've often felt the pressure to over-deliver in the workplace to prove I belonged. This was often at the expense of my health and wellness. When we overlay the intersectional dynamics of workplace bias and inequities with this conversation, it can be very easy to sit self-care on the back burner. Let's talk about some ways to ensure you prioritize self-care as a daily routine.

WHAT IS SELF-CARE?

Self-care is an inside job. What thoughts and actions are you practicing to be the best version of yourself today? Self-care is about knowing what/who best serves you and adjusting to make decisions aligned with your growth and goals. Self-care will change as you evolve and grow, so it's up to you to determine what it looks like in your life. The constant variable is that it's imperative. Like any other area of your work or business, self-care is necessary. It becomes even more critical as you navigate through change, challenge, and loss.

In NYC, I worked incessant 11–14-hour days. It became our way of life. Joe and I would leave around 8:00 a.m. to take the subway to work. On an early day, we'd have dinner right after work, still in our work clothes around 8 p.m. After a few months of this, I noticed my migraines were becoming more frequent. I was always tired even when I slept in to "make up for the week" on Saturdays. You know this doesn't work, right? I knew something had to give when I found myself waking up with excruciating neck pain that caused me to spend two nights in an NYC hospital for a spinal cord scare. This happened the day before I was supposed to be on the beach for my sorority sister's bachelorette trip. I went from a walk-in clinic X-ray to being immediately admitted to the hospital. Enough was enough. Here's what I had to ask myself:

- What aspects of my current routine serve me?
- Who is benefitting from my lack of alignment?
- Why am I not taking care of myself daily?
- How will I decide to do better daily?
- What changes do I need to make?
- Who will these changes impact?
- When will I have a conversation with those that I need to re-establish health boundaries or expectations with?

Hopefully, it won't take a health scare for you to realize you are your greatest asset. Your self-care starts with you! What's happening inside gets expressed outside. Sometimes we can over-index on the image of self-care rather than the intent of it. We must go beyond the surface of spa days and salon visits to prioritize the substance of our self-awareness, beliefs, and renewal to be well mentally, emotionally, and physically. Let's briefly discuss these core areas of inner self-care:

SELF-AWARENESS IS NECESSARY

When is the last time you spent time getting to know you? I know this seems like a weird question. But at the core of what makes good leaders exceptional is self-awareness. In my coaching programs, the first place we start is self-awareness. How do you see yourself and acknowledge your thoughts, feelings, desires, and aspirations? One of the frameworks I use to coach clients through this process is knowing your **VISA**. Now, this isn't about a credit card, but similar to the card, it's everywhere you want to be! One of the goals of being more self-aware is to align with opportunities representing who you are. If you're a client or have heard me speak about the power of introspection, intention, and implementation before, then you will know **VISA** is an acronym for:

- **VALUES** – What are your non-negotiables that are the lens through which you make decisions?
- **INTERESTS** – What are you curious about? What do you do when you have discretionary time?
- **SKILLS** – What capabilities have you invested time or money to develop?
- **ABILITIES** – What are your strengths? What capabilities come easy to you? What are your gifts?

When you're clear on your **values, interests, skills, and abilities,** it helps you thrive in your life, career, and business. You will communicate with more confidence and clarity. You will also have a clear point of reference for making decisions on opportunities aligned with who you are. This is especially helpful when you're experiencing change, challenge, and loss. Your **VISA** becomes a guide for decision making in moments like this. Self-awareness is a cornerstone of emotional intelligence directly linked to your experience, discipline, and satisfaction in your relationships, career, and business.

> *When you're clear on your values, interests, skills, and abilities, it helps you thrive in your life, career, and business.*

INTROSPECTION ACTIVITY

Here are some questions you can ask yourself to become a more self-aware leader:

1. What am I doing when I have the most joy?

2. When am I the best version of me?

3. How do I feel today? What do I need to release?

4. If I could change three specific things in my life right now, what would they be?

5. How would these changes make my life better?

6. When negative thoughts arise, what do I do?

7. What is working well in my business right now?

8. What motivates me to keep moving forward?

9. Who do I want to become?

10. What kind of person am I today?

11. What am I doing when it feels like time goes by fast?

12. What situations make me feel terrible?

13. What keeps me grounded when I feel overwhelmed?

14. What does it mean to me to do meaningful work?

BELIEVING IN YOURSELF

Now that you've committed to spending time to practice introspection, you will start to notice how what you believe frames how you think. I'll never forget the first time I was confronted with my self-sabotaging beliefs. I sat in Marshawn Evans Daniels' "Make Money Speaking" seminar, where I thought I would learn the strategies and tactics I needed to check off a list to become a professional speaker. Well, not only did I leave with that knowledge, but I also left with more wisdom and understanding around the power of belief and my own shrinking thinking.

There is so much I could share here. I know saying I gained more understanding around the power of belief sounds cliché. You may be thinking, "Well, yeah… duh!" I get it. I thought I had it together here, too. As a woman of faith who grew up the daughter of a pastor and always in church, I thought I had belief down! I didn't. One of the quickest ways to check your belief is to look at what you are (or aren't) building.

Belief is more than a psychological phenomenon; it's an action. Our decisions to go or not, stay or leave, ask or wait, leap or look, accept or decline, etc., are all grounded in what we believe to be true. This book is full of resources, and I hope you've gotten your *Thrive Through It* Toolkit brittanyncole.com/book. At the top of my list of recommended books to read or listen to is *Believe Bigger* by Marshawn Evans Daniels. This book and her teachings have changed my life. There isn't anyone better to teach you to believe bigger. She's a guru who will help you to elevate your belief, stop the "stinking, shrinking thinking," and silence "little me" so you can get on with the BIG dreams and plans you're destined to achieve. Visit believebigger.com to order your copy of the book and her companion devotional *100 Days of Believing Bigger*. We practice self-care by continuously believing in ourselves—even and especially when no one else does.

> *One of the quickest ways to check your belief is to look at what you are (or aren't) building. Belief is more than a psychological phenomenon; it's an action.*

REST FOR RENEWAL

The last way we go beyond the surface to make self-care a daily practice is by resting. Rest is critical to our natural need to renew our mind, body, and energy. As we discussed and know, we live in a culture that prioritizes the production over the producer. It can be easy to slip into a routine where we celebrate our external performance and results while neglecting our need for rest and renewal.

> *Rest is critical to our natural need to renew our mind, body, and energy.*

As a believer, I know rest is one of God's values. When we consider God's creation and how He created, we see periods of work followed by rest periods (see Genesis 2:3). As leaders, we must prioritize rest in our life, career, and business! Rest helps us to remain resilient as we reimagine, renew, and reinvent! When our commitment to work and being productive undermines our need to rest, we risk burnout, anxiety, and depression. The idea isn't to rest because we feel depleted to the point of exhaustion, but instead, rest to continue to be more efficient and show up at our best!

> *The idea isn't to rest because we feel depleted to the point of exhaustion, but instead, rest to continue to be more efficient and show up at our best!*

Here are some self-care resources to help you elevate your self-awareness, believe bigger, and rest for renewal

- Believe Bigger and 100 Days of Believing Bigger by Marshawn Evans Daniels
- A Sister's Siesta by Jasmin Forts
- The Memo by Minda Harts
- Ignite by Kelly D. Parker
- The Worthy Wardrobe by Morgan Wider

- Expect to Win by Carla Harris
- It's About Damn Time by Arlan Hamilton
- The Importance of Self Care playlist from TEDTalks

Here are some examples of self-care you can incorporate into your life. What would you add to this list?

- Ending work early to attend your child's game.
- Hiring help for your household maintenance.
- Taking a vacation day, even during your company's busy season.
- Taking your vacation days to schedule a staycation to recalibrate.
- Waking up an hour earlier to meditate and make breakfast.
- Scheduling and taking time to exercise.
- Asking for a promotion.
- Asking to be included in meetings or special projects.
- Speaking up in meetings, even if your voice shakes.
- Recognizing your team often and publicly.

Now you may find that the last one to be odd. How does your interaction with others help you to facilitate self-care? Let's talk about the connection between self-care and service.

SELF-CARE IS SERVICE

When we aren't useful to ourselves, we show up less optimally for the important people and projects in our lives. It can be challenging to think about self-care when we're facing change, challenge, and loss. However, it's in these moments where we have to be most attentive to how we're taking care of ourselves. We can't pour from an empty cup. Even if you think your cup isn't empty, we all know there's a difference in the pour from a full cup and one we have to turn completely over to get anything out of. As we're serving as leaders in ministry, our organizations, and our family, our effectiveness as servant leaders hinges on how well we take care of ourselves. As the saying goes, what's inside the cup is for you, and the overflow is for other people.

We discussed how rest is a core value to God, and there are many Biblical references to Jesus sleeping and retreating to rest. The idea of self-care and recognizing our daily need to rest isn't just about our self-interest. It also ensures we show up better for others as we take time to:

- Practice introspection.
- Prioritize personal development and manage our mindset.
- Connect with others to cultivate a community where we can thrive.

Self-care isn't selfish. In many ways, it's selfless because the return on the investment to prioritize our wellbeing, benefits those around us. The more we fill our cup, the more we have to pour into others. One of the valuable lessons I've learned about self-care as a leader is that it's critical to exemplify the behaviors and boundaries of the team. For example, if I say to my team, "Don't worry about responding to emails on the weekend." Yet I'm sending emails over the weekend; it sends the wrong message. Although I've said one thing, my actions are communicating the opposite. So regardless of my intention, when my team receives the email notification, the impact will be pressure about whether or not to respond.

Self-care that sets and maintains boundaries is often in service to those around you and those who come behind you. This is what I reminded myself when I went back to NYC to work after my mom's funeral and determined whether or not to have a crucial conversation with Ryan. From my perspective, Ryan had overstepped and violated my trust.

> *Self-care that sets and maintains boundaries is often in service to those around you and those who come behind you.*

Rather than sharing his concerns with me, he told me I was doing a great job and spoke to my former skip-level leader about his challenges working with me. I decided I would say something. At this point, my initial disappointment and frustration with the situation were gone. However, I couldn't get two things out of my mind:

1. What if he thinks this behavior is okay? I try to always err on the side of extending grace. Despite what I know about bias and inequities in the workplace, I thought perhaps there's a slim chance no one has ever brought up his lack of emotional intelligence, empathy, or communication skills. Maybe he really thought this behavior was ok. So, regardless of my discomfort, this could be a great learning opportunity for him.

The second and more prominent question I couldn't get out of my mind was:

2. What if he treats the next Black woman on his team like this? Deep down in my heart, I didn't believe he had ill intentions. My gut instinct was he thought the way he managed our first few months of working together was okay. So, if I didn't speak up and moved on, potentially there would be someone else in my position dealing with the same subpar leadership. I couldn't get past this one.

I decided to have the crucial conversation. Although I was initially extremely uncomfortable, nervous, and overly analytical in my preparation, the discussion went exceptionally well. I asked my manager to help me understand his thought process around not sharing his detailed feedback directly with me. I shared my experience of our first few months working together and everything that had been happening back at home with my mom. We both left the conversation grateful, relieved, and, most importantly, more aware, and better connected as colleagues. It was one of those moments where you can feel the weight lifting off your shoulders. From that conversation on, I thrived in that position working on Ryan's team. Not only did the conversation improve my well-being and understanding, but it was also in service to Ryan and all those who work with him to this day.

Self-care is service, and service is a sustainability strategy. As the African proverb states, "If you want to go fast, go alone; but if you want to go far, go together." Sometimes going together and helping people get together is inconvenient, particularly when experiencing our own trauma and pain. It may feel more comfortable to retreat and focus only on you, but I want to encourage you to keep showing up and keep serving. Serving is the gateway for renewing your mind and spirit, leading to positive wellbeing, substantive connections, and even promotion.

> *Serving is the gateway for renewing your mind and spirit, leading to positive wellbeing, substantive connections, and even promotion.*

SERVICE IS A SUSTAINABILITY STRATEGY

Serving isn't an activity; it's an approach to life. Often when we think about serving, one of the first things to come to mind is participating in a service event. Whether you're a member of an organization focused on community service such as my illustrious Sorors of Delta Sigma Theta Sorority, Inc. or you plan and participate in your own community service activities, opportunities to give back are endless. One of the most challenging aspects of resilience is how to sustain the grit and fortitude despite the challenges over time. Serving helps us maintain a sense of purpose, peace, and perspective through our change, challenge, and loss.

It was one of the saddest mornings ever. July 20, 2018, I'll never forget, was a Friday morning. Joe and I were in Manhattan, getting ready for work. We usually left at the same time. Right as we were about to leave, Joe's phone rang. He walked over to the couch to sit down, and I knew that the news wasn't good as he talked to his best friend. Their one-year-old son, our godson, had died. I immediately started looking for flights from New York to Memphis for us to get there Friday evening at the latest while Joe still talked to Jon Bond. Jackson was unexpectedly diagnosed with a rare form of cancer approximately four months prior. Before his diagnosis, he was a healthy baby and had just celebrated his first birthday two weeks before his death. Despite our open wounds, crazy schedules at work, and astronomical airfare prices to fly the same day to Memphis, we didn't think twice. We were clearing one hurdle at a time, whatever it took to be there with them.

When we got to Memphis, it felt like I was having an out-of-body experience. I couldn't believe it. Our friends, Jonathan and Victoria, were so strong in the Lord and were encouraging us. As we sat with them, I was reminded of God's sovereignty. I began to feel so grateful that we could be present with them through this. We thought we were there for them, to be present and supportive as they mourned their beautiful baby boy. All the while, they were the ones lifting us. I'm sure you can relate to this occurrence when it comes to serving others. Many service experiences work this way. You end up leaving with so much more than you came for. The people you think you're "helping" end up helping you. We only experience this when we prioritize others. As we helped them with funeral plans over the next few days and prepared the last thing baby Jackson would wear, there were so many flashbacks of my mom's preparation. Despite my initial concern about how I would manage this, serving his parents lifted my spirits, and their light encouraged us through it.

Service—even during loss—helps to elevate our focus. We become more aware of the bigger opportunity around us and the privilege to be a source of love, grace, and support for someone else. Often one of the best ways to thrive through loss is to extend grace to embody the very thing you believe you need. There is so much power in being what you need. If you need support, be supportive of someone else. If you need a listening ear, be a listening ear for someone else. If you need love, show love to

> *Service—even during loss—helps to elevate our focus. Often one of the best ways to thrive through loss is to extend grace to embody the very thing you believe you need.*

someone else. There is this miraculous shift in your mental capacity and emotional wellbeing when you serve others' needs while being for other people what you believe you need for yourself. Here are some fantastic organizations you can connect with to support through service:

- The African American Leadership Forum
- The American Heart Association
- Saved in the City
- INROADS
- YWCA
- The Next Door
- Black Girls Code
- The National Sales Network
- The Equity Alliance
- Second Harvest Food Bank
- Big Brother Big Sisters

SERVE THROUGH IT

As you're considering ways to serve others to thrive through it, don't forget about the critical value of being of service to yourself. Self-care isn't self-indulgence; it's service. When we're aware of what we need and operate from a position of purpose, we're at our best for those around us. As we become clearer on our identity, reimagined priorities, and ways to reinvent, it can be scary to go after exactly what we want. We can quickly find ourselves in analysis paralysis, trying to identify our next best move. I want to encourage you to harness that fear in service to yourself and those around you. Show up, even through loss. Speak up, even through loss. Serve with purpose, even through loss.

> *Show up, even through loss. Speak up, even through loss. Serve with purpose, even through loss.*

Audre Lorde says it best in the 1977 speech, "The Transformation of Silence into Language and Action."

"When I dare to be powerful—to use my strength in the service of my vision—then it becomes less and less important whether I am afraid... I must speak the truth as I see it and share not just my triumphs, not just the things that felt good, but the pain. The intense, often unmitigated pain. It is important to share how I know survival is survival and not just a walk through the rain."

I've had to learn that speaking up, sharing my truth, and staying true to my vision isn't just self-care. It's resilient service.

In quarter three of 2018, I was tapped about a sales management opportunity back in Nashville. I was in my marketing role in NYC and had begun the conversations around my next promotion and thought it would be in NYC, expanding my brand management experience. The timing was sooner than planned and it was a sales leader role instead of a marketing role, however this opportunity was too aligned to pass up. I applied and aced the final interview on a Friday. The following Monday I was offered the interim position and asked to start the next day. Yes, it was that fast. Since at the time I led the majority of the marketing assets that were priorities the following year for our brand, I ended up working out a plan to spend the first two months in my new role flying back and forth between New York and Nashville. A few weeks into this arrangement, I was at a national sales launch meeting in October 2018. This was my first meeting with my new team, and I was excited! The morning of my first meeting with the new team, I was informed the role I'd just accepted would last five months instead of eighteen, and not to mention this to my new team. I practiced a lot of thought-stopping that day to get through the rest of the trip. A week later, I was back in NYC and was informed my marketing role (that was considered my "full time" role while I was working as interim role and the one I would return to after the interim role was up) would be eliminated at the same time my interim role ended. This meant I'd be in a layoff wave as the company restructured. In less than two months, I went from meetings about my next marketing role to being on a layoff list with a clock ticking in our flattening organization.

Amid these unexpected circumstances, I was still leading my new sales team that was number one in the region, as if everything was normal after being asked not to share my news with them. The entire organization was in transition, and the sales organization would have layoffs soon as well. I tapped into every mental toughness strategy I knew and prioritized serving my team and showing up to be a resource and add value to help them elevate and achieve more – both individually and as a team. We had change management workshops, countless 1:1 coaching conversations; holiday festivities; celebrations for a teammates' promotion; and leading performance milestone recognitions. I was having conversations on field rides about the potential impact of layoffs while I was in that exact boat myself. Every day I would set aside time to either look for roles, connect with a colleague on opportunities, or just think through my options. Outside of this scheduled "me time" of thirty minutes to an hour, I put all of my focus on supporting and serving my team. It helped me remain positive, focused, purposeful, and intentional with my energy and mindset, despite having many more questions than answers.

Carla Harris is one of my favorite speakers. When she speaks about organizational change, she promotes keeping one's head up and being intentional and proactive to provide solutions for gaps. I believe this is such great advice as there is always opportunity connected to change, regardless of how challenging it is. This is precisely what I did. In addition to my day roles, I served as the lead on highly visible diversity, equity, and inclusion projects through our employee resource groups (ERGs). Although I worked on impactful programs and initiatives, they weren't sustainable. All the leaders had day jobs, and we were working through the night and on weekends to support our ERG responsibilities. I decided to develop a plan for a more integrated and aligned strategy across all ERGs that would track, measure, and optimize all the activity that was taking place. At that time, each ERG worked in a silo, so there was much duplication. Due to the lack of strategy, there was little to no acknowledgment of intersectionality across the groups. I put my deck together, gathered stakeholders for feedback and alignment and got buy-in across the board from most leaders. This included engaging with the senior leader who owned the business unit's budget and would make the final decision. It all came to a screeching halt when I was told in the worst demeaning and disrespectful tone by a HR leader that I was "everywhere" and needed to focus on finding a job. Rumors began to swirl that I would be helping with diversity recruiting for the organization. However, after several meetings with the manager I'd be reporting to, it was clear the scope of the role didn't include diverse talent sourcing. Can you say confusion? That was exactly what this was. Between leading my team; searching for opportunities; creating an opportunity that got canned; feeling like I was baited and switched on what could've been a great opportunity; and the growing tug that there was more I was meant to be and do—I decided to bet on myself. During the crucial conversations, confusion, and clutter, I had to embody that quote by Audre Lorde and "be powerful—to use my strength in the service of my vision." That's exactly what I decided to do and made some bold moves despite fear.

What made this experience even more challenging is that I had the support of many colleagues who were aware of my predicament. A couple leaders I didn't even know knew my name approached me to find a way to "keep me on the bus." I knew my value was seen and felt, and I appreciated that. I also knew those last 3–6 months were stressful, unclear, and uncomfortable to say the least. I recognized these were signs to take the leap. I weighed every option and found it would've been easier to stay, even while working with some challenging colleagues. Instead, I decided to serve my team to the best of my ability and to speak up, show up, and "dare to be powerful" in service to myself. You are your best advocate in the workplace. My self-care to take the leap into entrepreneurship has been a daily lesson in service. I am better because of it and feel blessed to be building Career Thrivers and serving some of the most outstanding clients! Where will your self-care take you? "The greatest among you must be a servant" (Matthew 23:11, NLT).

Thoughts along the journey:

7. Be What You Need

1. What are your top three needs right now?

2. How would your life be better if these needs were met? List each need and the corresponding life or business improvement.

3. How can you serve others in this way?

4. Choose two areas of focus for serving this month. List them here and schedule on your calendar how and when you will serve.

5. How will you incorporate self-care into your everyday life?

6. Make a list of affirmations below. Choose three to share and affirm other people in your life.

CHAPTER 8

Supporting Others Through Loss

It's not about you. How do they feel they need to be supported?

As we redefine resilience, we are acknowledging our humanity, the seasons of change in our lives, and the requirement of rest. We are not risking burnout to prove how strong we are. As we've discussed, resilience is less about bouncing back and more aligned with how we extrapolate the lessons from our loss to reimagine and reinvent our lives and business in new ways. As a result of the change, challenge, or loss you've experienced, you show up differently. Your mindset has shifted. Your values have taken center stage. Boundaries protect your priorities. As you journey forward through The Resilience Roadmap® you create a more profound sense of who you are, why you're here, and who you want to become. Give yourself space and grace to learn, unlearn, and relearn as you journey through. This will help you discover what you need now and how to share so others can support you.

Give yourself space and grace to learn, unlearn, and relearn as you journey through.

ACCEPTING SUPPORT AND RECEIVING GRACE

When our focus through adversity is centered around bouncing back or returning to where and how we were before the loss, it can cause us to form a façade around how we're coping. One of the initial ways we accept support and receive grace is by substituting "I'm fine" with an authentic acknowledgment of our feelings. As my therapist shared with me, fine is not a feeling. This may seem like a small act to remove this general response from our vocabulary, but overtime ignoring our feelings and the support we need can harm us mentally, emotionally, and even physically as burnout sets in. I'm not saying we become helpless or hopeless in our response to adversity. However, I suggest we pause long enough to be more aware of how grief impacts us as we navigate an authentic journey through this new time in our lives. Your journey through The Resilience Roadmap® says, "Okay. I'm walking through this new journey and I am:

> *One of the initial ways we accept support and receive grace is by substituting "I'm fine" with an authentic acknowledgment of our feelings.*

- Acknowledging how I'm feeling,
- Identifying the loss,
- Revealing where I am with those around me so I can deal and heal,
- Okay with being uncomfortable as I have new emotions and experiences,
- Having some tough conversations,
- Reimaging to reinvent,
- Being what I need through self-care and service.
- Now I'm ready to share the load!"

What does sharing the load look like? Sharing the load requires us to be vulnerable in ways often counter to our socialized approach of hiding our pain to get over grief. Brene' Brown shares in her viral TED talk, "Vulnerability sounds like truth and feels like courage. Truth and courage aren't always comfortable, but they are never weaknesses." When we are vulnerable about our experiences through loss, we can engage and learn from the wise counsel of others. Much can be said about how people support others through loss regarding what they choose to say. We will discuss this in a moment. Before we get there, though, we must be willing to share where we are and let others in to support our journey through.

> *Sharing the load requires us to be vulnerable in ways often counter to our socialized approach of hiding our pain to get over grief.*

This has been a challenging rest stop for me on this Resilience Roadmap®. I grew up the youngest of three and the only girl. As a young athlete, I was taught the importance of tenacity. You're taught to have grit! Sore? Not feeling your best? Athletes suck it up and move along. I mean, let's think about it. Some of the greatest NBA players' stories are connected to how they overcame pain or illness to win. My experience as an athlete also taught me some of these principles and followed me into the workplace. Despite traumatic experiences, the pain of loss, and even illness on some occasions, I was taught I had to be strong, prove I was capable, and work twice as hard to get half as much. This mindset and even mantra of working twice as hard to get half as much has been birthed out of the inequalities and inequities across the history of the United States. As a result, this lesson has resounded in the homes of many Black families and becomes the lens by which many Black professionals view career aspirations.

So much of my life—from being the only girl on the junior pro basketball team to the only Black girl on an AAU girls' basketball team to the youngest and only Black woman in a boardroom—has been shaped by this need to power through circumstances. This show of strength is often meant to prove I belong. It can make vulnerability seem foreign or out of reach due to bias, discrimination, and racism. Although this is true for many, I believe more than one thing can be true at the same time. While systems and corporate cultures need to be restructured and cultivated to intentionally include differences, I believe I do a disservice to myself and women who look like me when I wear the cape and the mask to prove I'm strong and that I belong.

The paradigm of working twice as hard to get half as much is now problematic for me. Part of this revelation, in doing the work to unpack my vulnerability, was acknowledging I was afraid of showing up as myself because my experiences in corporate America conditioned me to code switch. I wore the armor. However, to receive the love, grace, and support from those around me, they had to know I needed it. Oh, and I needed it! As I began to lean into vulnerability and share exactly where I was regardless of my environment, my colleagues, close friends, and family showed up for me in ways that lifted some of the weight off my shoulders. On an episode of Oprah's Super Soul Sunday on OWN, Brene' Brown says it like this, "Vulnerability is not about fear and grief and disappointment. It is the birthplace of everything we are hungry for." (Winfrey, 2019) How will you open up and share to accept support and receive grace? Although many workplaces have a long way to go to cultivate the culture that makes authenticity seamless for all, I do believe that showing up fully and using your voice authentically helps in those hard moments.

Own your development. Own your story. Use your voice.

When we model real resilience amid adversity, we aren't trying to construct this narrative or a false sense of the reality of what we should be doing or how we should be experiencing life. Instead, we're journeying through with courageous vulnerability about where we are and what we need, allowing people to show up for us. We can't say we don't have the support we need if we aren't honest about the areas where we need support. When we do this, it allows people to make a clear decision on how they can support us through loss.

HOW TO SUPPORT OTHERS THROUGH IT

We've all been there. We get the news that someone we know and love is going through a tragedy, change, or loss. We know that they are experiencing a range of emotions from sadness to anger to perhaps even guilt. Some of the most challenging questions to answer in moments when we have a family member, friend, or colleague experiencing a loss is usually "what do I say" and "what can I do?" I believe there are many answers to these questions. Here are my thoughts on how you can A.C.T. to support others through it.

AWARENESS – Understand how grief can impact others. As we discussed in Chapter 1, there isn't one set process or way to grieve. Grief is one of the most complex, unpredictable, and all-encompassing emotions we face. People experience a rollercoaster of emotions in a matter of moments that can seem extreme but are likely how they process their pain. Understanding this will help manage expectations and refrain from expecting how one "should" respond. Just as we commit not to should ourselves as we're grieving, let's also refrain from shoulding others. Be aware that grief has no time limit and looks different on every person. Therefore, don't attempt to divert. In Martha Hickman's book, Healing After Loss: Daily Meditations for Working Through Grief, she says, "It is probably well-meaning – this attempt to help a mourner 'think of something else,' 'get your mind off it.' As though we could think of something else when grief is fresh. The well-meaning attempt may also be the comforter's uneasiness about what to say. Never mind that a supporting listening presence is more important than the right words."

COMMUNICATION – Have you ever been nervous about bringing up the loss someone has experienced because you don't want to bring them down? Depending on the nature of the loss, ignoring it could seem like you're ignoring them. Don't allow your fear of knowing exactly what to say to keep you from reaching out. There's no need to shift the conversation to something "happy." It's okay to acknowledge the loss has occurred. Instead of being concerned about what to say, focus on displaying compassion and asking questions that position you to listen and share your presence and availability. Express your concern genuinely and create space for the person grieving to share as much or as little as they would like with you at that moment. Once they share, remember your role isn't to critique

> *Instead of being concerned about what to say, focus on displaying compassion and asking questions that position you to listen and share your presence and availability.*

their response, relate to it, or solve it. Lastly, a final reminder, remove the word "at least" from your vocabulary; it minimizes the other person's emotions.

WHAT TO SAY:

Listen more than you speak.

Acknowledge the loss - "John shared with me that your mom died. I can't imagine how you are feeling."

Express your care and concern - "I'm sorry you're hurting, and I'm here for you."

Ask if the person feels like talking - "Are you ok to talk? What is on your mind right now?"

Be genuine and transparent - "I'm not sure what to say. But I want you to know I care, and I'm here for you."

Nothing - Be okay sitting in silence and offering a reassuring shoulder squeeze, hug, or back rub.

Ask about the loved on that died - "What is one of your favorite memories of your mother?"

Instead of "Let me know if..." an alternative could be - "I'm going to the grocery store this evening. What can I bring you from there?" "I ordered you some groceries. When can I drop them off?"

WHAT **NOT** TO SAY:

Don't minimize what they're feeling - "At least you/they…"

Don't try to reason or solve their problems - Allow them to express themselves without judgment or critique.

Religious platitudes are often devoid of empathy or emotional intelligence - "This is God's plan. He needed her." Please don't say this.

Redirecting to gratitude or "positive" comments - "Look at how long she was here. You have so much to be thankful for."

Comparing the person's grief to yours or anyone else's - "At least she saw you get married. My mom died when I was in college."

TIMING – Often, when we hear someone we know has experienced loss, we immediately reach out to the person. In the first week after my mom's death, I was inundated with calls and texts that I was in no position to receive fully. That's not to say I didn't appreciate the immediate responders. I did, and so did our family. The well-wishes from family, friends, and co-workers were a source of strength. In addition to that, it's essential to consider the timing associated with loss. At times I think it's better to wait and share your thoughts a week or even two weeks after getting "the news." Grief continues long after the initial moments of loss and mourning. When a loved one dies, there's an endless wave of texts, calls, card, etc. in those first few days and then a couple weeks later, silence. What's even more interesting to me is that for many reasons, those first few days are often the worst times to drop food by, call, come over, etc. The family is mourning and has the pressure to plan a funeral service for their loved one all while hosting family and friends and receiving meal after meal. Yes, all of the gestures are kind. However, it has always seemed odd the way we rush to show up for people initially when often times they need our presence the most after the crowd is gone and the impact of the loss sets in. Although it can be comforting for people to reach out in the early moments, it can be even more meaningful to continue supporting and checking in with friends and family in the weeks, months, and even years later. When you think of that person—even if it's not a holiday–reach out and share, you were thinking of them. I can't tell you how many moments I received random messages like this that were breaths from heaven and kept me going. That call, card, text, drop by, etc., months after the initial loss can mean the world!

These are some practical ways you can ACT to support others through it. Keep in mind that we don't always have to prioritize doing something big to show our support. In many moments, making the sacrifice to simply be there is enough. Sometimes our best action is to be present and willing to inconvenience ourselves in order to show up for others when they need it most. One of the ways we do this in the workplace is through allyship. As we've discussed, career grief is real and when coupled with the emotional tax of being Black in the workplace, it's helpful to have allies that are aware and also willing to take action.

> *Sometimes our best action is to be present and willing to inconvenience ourselves in order to show up for others when they need it most.*

THE AWARENESS AND ACTIONS OF ALLIES ®

With the continued racial injustice in the United States in 2020, many of us found ourselves grieving the murders of Breonna Taylor, Ahmaud Arbery, and George Floyd at the hands of police. Despite the renewed energy around racial justice, this was not the first time that Black lives were snatched away, with video evidence, at the hands of those sworn to protect and serve. However, there were many firsts that swept across corporate, non-profit, and government workplaces. For the first time, many organizations hosted companywide conversations and shared external communications on race, justice, and equity. While I believe the intentions of most of these organization reactions were positive, many of them fell short on both communicating why (purpose) equity is important and how (strategy) they plan to address it.[13]

Like many Black professionals, I received more apologies than I could count. From email to social media, there were streams of regretful acknowledgment of indirect offenses from friends and strangers alike on behalf of our failed law enforcement system in the killings of Breonna Taylor, Ahmaud Arbery, and George Floyd. These were a new set of names, but these stories ended the same and left many Black Americans struggling between grief and gratitude. On the one hand, I was grateful for the awakening happening in communities and companies across the country. At the same time, I also was frustrated at the high cost of this acknowledgment. In addition to that, the real question is, what do we do

---

[13] Ruchika Tulshyan. Do Your Employees Know Why You Believe in Racial Equity? Harvard Business Review. June 30, 2020. https://hbr.org/2020/06/do-your-employees-know-why-you-believe-in-racial-equity

once we move from apology to agreement and enough is enough? Enter the allies roll call.

Before we discuss the actions of allies, let's first align on some important definitions. An ally is recognized by a community as someone who is engaged in intentional learning and taking action to advance the inclusion and equity of that community. Allyship is a process that requires both awareness and action of those with more privilege and power to empathize with and advocate for marginalized communities of people. We don't arrive at a self-determined destination and then self-identify as allies. Allyship is a journey of learning, un-learning, and re-learning as we show our support by sharing the load of another. If you've never taken an uncomfortable action, you likely aren't seen as an ally. Allyship is about sharing your power and privilege especially when it's uncomfortable.

> *An ally is recognized by a community as someone who is engaged in intentional learning and taking action to advance the inclusion and equity of that community.*

> *Allyship is a journey of learning, un-learning, and re-learning as we show our support by sharing the load of another. Allyship is about sharing your power and privilege especially when it's uncomfortable.*

One of my favorite explanations of allyship is from Roxane Gay, author of Bad Feminist. In a 2016 article (these aren't new 2020 problems) in Marie Claire, "On Making Black Lives Matter," Roxane shares:

> *"Black people do not need allies. We need people to stand up and take on the problems borne of oppression as their own without remove or distance. We need people to do this even if they cannot fully understand what it's like to be oppressed for their race or ethnicity, gender, sexuality, ability, class, religion, or other marker of identity. We need people to use common sense to figure out how to participate in social justice."[14]*

In short, it's time for non-BIPOC professionals to move from words to actions.

This is why I created our Career Thrivers curriculum: **The Awareness and Actions of Allies** ®. I believe leaders have a responsibility to move from apologies and passive communications to action-focused and productive change. This is what supporting Black and Brown colleagues within your organization looks like. Yes, this will be uncomfortable. Mistakes are inevitable. It will cost you something. Yet, this is the work of allyship.

> *Leaders have a responsibility to move from apologies and passive communications to action-focused and productive change.*

---

[14] Roxane Gay. On Making Black Lives Matter. Marie Claire. July 11, 2016. https://www.marieclaire.com/culture/a21423/roxane-gay-philando-castile-alton-sterling/

As leaders, we welcome discomfort because being uncomfortable is a prerequisite for growth. As allies, we must be intentional to move past getting defensive due to discomfort to take on the actions of:

o   Speaking up when our voice shakes.
o   Taking a stand when we're scared.
o   Holding the door open to share our access and privilege even when we aren't sure.

This work isn't about our good intentions, it's about impact. You may feel discomfort and even pain in doing this, but to borrow the first line of Rick Warren's best-selling book, The Purpose-Driven Life, "It's not about you." Here is an overview of our workshop and course that equips working professionals and leaders on the actions of **A.L.L.I.E.S.:**

> *This work isn't about our good intentions, it's about impact.*

THE AWARENESS AND ACTIONS OF ALLIES®

A – AWARENESS: Emotional intelligence is critical for allyship. Do the work to understand and challenge your implicit bias. "Why do I think that" is a great question to be more self-aware when thoughts enter your mind about other people, particularly those who are different than you.

L – LEARNING: Don't expect those that are marginalized and/or grieving to teach you what you haven't been intentional in learning about on your own first. It's great to listen and ask questions, continue to do this as you are also doing your own research to know, be, and do better.

L – LISTENING: Suppress the urge to counter with your ideas and experiences. Listen more than you speak and know that allyship isn't about wearing a cape. No one needs to be saved, but everyone needs to be understood. Awareness, learning, and listening will enhance your understanding to take action.

I – INCLUSION: How are you intentional in your effort to incorporate difference? As leaders, having diversity in your organization isn't enough. Diversity (difference) is all around us, even if your organization needs to recruit more diversity. The real question is, how are you cultivating a culture of inclusion where those who are different believe they belong, so you retain them? Diversity is a fact, inclusion is an act, and equity is in the stats.

E – EXPERIENCE: What has your experience been with people who are different from you? How intentional are you in experiencing the breadth and depth of Black culture? In addition, how has your experience changed? Allyship will cost you your comfort at the very least. If you aren't taking a risk publicly to share your power with the people you want to be an ally for then it's likely that the work you think you're doing is performative.

S – SPONSORSHIP: Use your power and privilege to empower and position BIPOC founders, colleagues, politicians, and leaders. For example, how do you speak up and invest in the Black people you're sharing experiences with, especially when you're in rooms they are not in?

This is what allyship looks like. It's more than support and it's certainly more than nice sentiments. What sacrifice are you making to walk the talk of allyship? These are the actions of allies that will create meaningful change in our schools, non-profits, corporations, small businesses, and even our government.

The social media posts are nice—whether genuine or performative. However, our awareness and action are necessary. Every day we have an opportunity to practice allyship. Every experience is an opportunity for continuous improvement. The apologies will be plentiful on this journey of supporting others— —especially supporting people who are different than us. Get comfortable being uncomfortable and let your actions speak of the change you want to see in the world.

> *Get comfortable being uncomfortable and let your actions speak of the change you want to see in the world.*

LEVELS OF SUPPORT

One of my most memorable moments of support in the workplace happened with a marketing leader when I was living in NYC and got the call about my mom the morning of Monday, June 5, 2017. After getting helped back on my feet from the security staff in the lobby, I made it up the elevator and into her office. I was crying and sharing that I needed to leave and get to Nashville right away and wasn't sure when I'd be back. She asked me to sit down, stopped what she was doing, and immediately booked me a flight. I remember the compassion and concern she shared to make sure I got home that day, even using her positional authority with our travel team to ensure I had the best flight option to get a non-stop flight out of New York and into Nashville.

To this day, I don't know if she paid for the plane ticket or if my company did. Either way, I know I never handed her a card, and she never asked me about payment for that very expensive same-day flight out of LaGuardia airport. She saw what I needed and swiftly went about removing barriers for me. She booked my flight, communicated with our team, and worked with my admin to take care of the back-to-back meetings on my calendar that week and beyond. I'm forever grateful for how she supported me that day and beyond. Her kindness and the thoughtful support of my colleagues throughout those early weeks after my mother's death, helped me make the hard decision to return to NYC.

Often when I'm coaching clients one-on-one through their career and leadership journey, I share about the necessity of building relationships. Having the support of others is essential for thriving in any area of life. From advocating on your behalf to reach your next role, to sharing the load of your loss, our success is inextricably linked to the people around us.

I believe there are four key levels of support and that it's necessary to properly identify where people are in order to manage expectations around the kind of support you will receive from them. I use a map to help me identify who is in my network and a pyramid to categorize where people are and in

> *The clearest sign of support is investment.*

what areas I need to strengthen my relationships. How do you know who supports you? The clearest sign of support is investment.

Monetary investment is often the initial thought when we hear this word, but when it comes to having support from others, time and expertise investments are also important. Ensuring you have properly identified and have breadth at each level is what makes a strong support system. When someone truly supports your career, a cause, your business, or you, there is no question because they invest their time, talent and finances. Let's take a look at each of the levels!

PYRAMID OF SUPPORT

SPONSORS

SUPPORTERS

↑ —— INVESTORS —— ↑

ENCOURAGERS

SPECTATORS

SPECTATORS – *"Hey, it's good to see you!"*

These are the people who see you. Sometimes you know they see you and most of the time you don't. **Spectators are the largest group in your network and thus the base that we build from.** This is important to keep in mind because oftentimes we use the word "spectators" with a negative connotation. However, this level is critical because these people are observing your moves, taking mental notes of your results, assessing your attitude, reading your captions and blog posts and are very much aware of who you are. They may even engage with you in some way that's visible. Spectators are a good group to get feedback from because they will be the most unbiased of your level of support and because they're watching, they can share valuable insight with you. Engage your spectators and they will shift.

ENCOURAGERS – *"Keep up the great work!"*

This is the group of people who affirm you. They provide positive feedback and can truly be a motivation and inspiration in the workplace or in your business. Encouragers don't wait for the mid or end of year review, they consistently look for moments to lift you up with a kind word. Although this group in your network can be a source of strength, it can also be a level where mismanaged expectations happen. Oftentimes, the people we are disappointed in because they didn't "support" us are encouragers. They have positively affirmed us, so we have an assumed expectation of what that means. This is why I say the clearest sign of support is investment; **and investment is the difference between encouragers and supporters.**

SUPPORTERS – *"How can I help you?"*

Now we've crossed over to the investors in our network. **Supporters are people who actively engage with you by sharing their time, talent, and/or treasure to help you reach your goals.** These are the people who offer or agree to write a recommendation, help you plan your event, give you advice on how to navigate a challenge, make time for you quarterly for mentorship, purchase a ticket to your event, etc. If you're not clear on whether someone supports you, they are likely in the encourager category because this group is making a clear investment in you. Many people's network ends here with supporters, but if you're going to advance your career or grow your business you absolutely need this last level.

SPONSORS – *"I spoke with the hiring manager on your behalf today."*

I use a pyramid to visibly represent these levels because you will have less people in each level as you move up and that is okay. You don't need and likely won't have the same number of sponsors as supporters. What is a sponsor? Think of it like this, supporters will save you a seat at the meeting and a sponsor will have an additional chair brought into their meeting to make room for you to sit down. **Sponsors have the positional power to create opportunities for you and speak up on your behalf in rooms you don't have**

access to. They are supporters with influence, power, and access and they share that with you. One of the best explanations on the difference between mentors and sponsors is Carla Harris' viral 2018 TED talk "How to Find the Person Who Can Help You Get Ahead at Work." I include a link to this in the Thrive Through It Toolkit, so be sure to sign up for your free gift at brittanyncole.com/book.

INVESTING IN SUPPORT

There are times when despite having an amazing pyramid of support with spectators and sponsors you want, there are still gaps. This is where investment comes in. There are many different types of investments—financial, intellectual, relational, etc. Regardless of the area, the core principle of investing is to allocate a valued resource with an expectation of generating a higher return. In our life and business, we typically think of financial investments where we allocate capital in order to gain a profitable ROI–return on investment. This doesn't always mean that we lack resources, but rather that we have an expectation that if we allocate the resources, we do have to a specific area it will yield more than we gave.

This same principle is true when it comes to living and leading with resilience. When I reflect on many of the stories I've shared with you in this book, both personal and professional, it was the investment in the specific support I needed at the time that helped me thrive through. When we're faced with change, challenges, and loss one of the best investments that we can make is in therapy. In fact, since experiencing the benefits of therapy, I believe this is an investment in support that is preventative in many ways. Likewise, investments I've made in coaching and consulting have also been very beneficial. Let's review each of these.

> *It was the investment in the specific support I needed at the time that helped me thrive through.*

INVESTING IN THERAPY

Therapy and coaching are not the same. Early in my grief journey with the death of my mother I can remember struggling with whether or not I "needed" a therapist. As believers, oftentimes ideas around faith and seeking help from a licensed healthcare provider are seen as either/or. I believe they are both/and. You can be a woman of faith, love the Lord, and have a standing appointment with a therapist. Therapy is a long-term process where you work with a healthcare provider to diagnose and resolve relationship challenges, beliefs, feelings, etc. that are problematic. Oftentimes with therapy you're reflecting on past trauma and experiences with guided introspection to help you create a more well and stable present and future. In an article titled "The Benefits and Options for Therapy in Healthline", Dr. Alex Klein outlines six types of therapy that include: talk therapy with a psychiatrist, psychologist, or therapist, individual therapy, family therapy, couples therapy, cognitive-behavioral therapy, and online therapy. Have you heard of the term psychotherapy? This is a technique that therapists use to facilitate their services across the different types of therapy.[15]

There are several resources available to shed light on the stigma around mental health and to access a more inclusive therapy and wellness experience. I've included a few below:

- **Therapy for Black Girls** – A site to help you search a therapist with content and podcast resources.

- **Shine** – A site and mobile app to help with mental healthcare and wellness representation and inclusion

- **The Boris Lawrence Henson Foundation** – Taraji P. Henson's organization to change the perception of mental illness in the Black community.

- **Ask Dr. Jess** – Information and resources with renowned psychiatrist, Dr. Jessica Clemons

- **Abundant Life Adventure Club** – A wellness community helping Black professionals maintain an active lifestyle through inclusive outdoor adventure.

    - **Triluna Wellness** – A pro-donut, non-diet, anti-racist wellness community.

---

[15] Dr. Alex Klein and Sara Lindberg. Benefits and Options for Therapy. Healthline. https://www.healthline.com/health/benefits-of-therapy

- **Heal Haus** – A Brooklyn based inclusive space for holistic health and wellness with diverse healing modalities and practitioners changing the stigma attached to healing.

In addition to these resources, I had the pleasure of connecting with two brilliant therapists to get their expert advice on thriving through grief.

Alethia J. Faison, MMFT
MARRIAGE AND FAMILY THERAPIST

MEET ALETHIA

Alethia J. Faison is a licensed Marriage and Family Therapist located in the Nashville, TN area. She's also a wife, mom, minister, and affectionately known as "Lady A" as the Leading Lady of Watson Grove Baptist Church (The Grove), a growing, multi-generational, multi-site church with campuses in Nashville, TN and Franklin, TN. One of my favorite things about Alethia is that she embraces her role as a faith leader to help destigmatize mental wellness within and beyond the Christian faith community. As a trained clinician, she specializes in helping you to learn healthy coping mechanisms that will aid you in navigating challenging life experiences without burning out or falling apart. Here's what she had to say about leveraging therapy to support your grief journey:

What is your advice on how to begin to journey forward after a loss?

Normalize your feelings. If you are sad honor that feeling. It represents a significant space or place someone or thing held in your life. It's okay to not be okay during this time. It's also okay to be okay during this time. Lean into your support system when you are ready, but take your time and go at "your" pace not someone else's expectation of what you should do and be after this loss.

What is the best way to support someone who is grieving?

Ask the person how you can support them. Oftentimes we think someone needs something while grieving when they don't. Give people who are grieving room and space to grieve but make it known that you are a resource of support when they are ready.

As you begin to create your next normal after loss, how do you manage possible feelings of guilt about "moving on?"

Those feelings may arise and it's okay. Deal with whatever guilt you may feel while walking on your journey to next. Just because you have feelings of guilt does not mean you can't move on or work towards healing. Every person is different and should do what feels right for them.

What additional advice would you like to share to help us thrive through it?

Know you are so capable of walking in a healed state. Deal with your feelings and emotions; get professional help if needed; and don't give up. Just because today is rough does not mean tomorrow can't be filled with joy and peace. Keep pushing! Your joy and peace may just await you on your journey. No matter what place you are in your life, there is still hope. Find your purpose and chase it! Live well while going through. You are so worth it!

What does thriving mean to you?

Thriving to me means recognizing your worth and know that no matter what you are enduring, you have made the decision that this is not your final chapter. Thriving through means walking into "Chapter Next!"

> To contact Alethia, please visit truththerapyinc.com or email alethiajfaison@truththerapyinc.com.

Rose Awotula Kehinde, GC-C
CERTIFIED GRIEF COUNSELOR

MEET ROSE

Rose Kehinde is a Certified Grief Counselor from the American Academy of Grief Counseling with experience working in the hospital and healthcare industry. She's also a wife, sister, aunt, and godmother. One of my favorite things about Rose is that she connects her personal experience and vulnerability with the death of her father to help people transform from healing to wholeness. Her transparency about her own functional depression and hard moments are experiences she openly shares to help others thrive through it. Here's what she had to say about journeying through grief and loss:

What is your advice on how to begin to journey forward after a loss?

My number one advice is to sit with the loss so there can be a true acknowledgment of what has happened. This may sound strange but, so often we want to "move on" by "staying busy" and moving about as if nothing has happened. Or we retreat into oneself not really acknowledging the loss. This causes room for depression to set in and/or the loss to hit a person at the most inopportune or unexpected time.

What is the best way to support someone that is grieving?

Personally, I advise people to be present. During times of bereavement, people often feel the need to say or do things when in fact, your presence is all that is required. The bereaved will tell you how they need you to support them. Checking in with them to make sure they are taking care of themselves physically is also helpful.

As you begin to create your next normal after loss, how do you manage possible feelings of guilt about "moving on?"

"Moving on" has a negative connotation. The reality is that you are continuing life. The loss experienced was a moment in your life that will shape your future. You continuing to live is not dishonoring that person, it is in fact an honor. It is important that we foster a mental culture that living after a loss is not disrespectful to that person's death.

What additional advice would you like to share to help us thrive through it?

Understand that the journey of grief is different for everyone, and we all handle loss in various ways. It is important that we seek help. This helps us with how to acknowledge the feelings and emotions that come along this journey. This defining moment is when you will discover a stronger, more resilient version of yourself.

The loss of my father, Dr. Samson Awotula was one that shook me deeply. I did everything I could to "move on" and be strong for everyone but myself. When it hit me what indeed had happened, I was already in a deep state of depression. I was a functional depressed person who had it all together in public but was breaking down daily behind closed doors. I hid all of this from my family and friends until one day, I couldn't anymore. I got help and spoke with a counselor and now I live life tapped into all the principles my father taught me. I use those conversations as my guide to rise through one of my darkest moments. I want to make him proud and I know that living my life with purpose does that!

What does thriving mean to you?

Simply put for me, thriving means rising in the darkest moment. Your determination to rise allows you to tap into parts of yourself that you didn't know existed until that hole was created.

To contact Rose please visit rosekehinde.com or email itscoachrosie@gmail.com.

As you can see from Alethia and Rose, therapy is a great way to help us get comfortable letting our guards down, personally and professionally, to show our wounds and allow others to support us through loss. It requires us to be honest, vulnerable, and transparent with a professional who can handle what we have to share. Therapy has helped me to practice vulnerability in a safe space so that I can show up with courage to be more vulnerable in spaces that may not initially have been safe to share my feelings. Vulnerability is strength and it creates trust, and trust is essential to thriving in relationships and business. Not only has therapy helped me to be more resilient as a leader, wife, daughter, and friend, coaching has also been a game changer for thriving personally and professionally.

INVESTING IN COACHING

As a reminder, therapy and coaching are not the same. As we discussed, therapy is a long-term approach that typically focuses in on understanding your past experiences to live a more joyful life with a licensed healthcare practitioner. Coaching on the other hand, is a process that is focused and short-term to help you improve your outcomes in a specific area. Coaching is more focused on what is happening today and helping you identify areas for improvement to get to where you want to be in the future.

Coaches help their clients identify clear goals and create an action plan to help with accountability towards reaching the client's desired results. Renowned speaker, author, coach, and philanthropist, Tony Robbins, has a great list of examples of when you would work with a coach and/or a therapist[16]:

A THERAPIST FOCUSES THEIR CONVERSATION ON WAYS TO:

- Recover from past traumas

---

[16] Tony Robbins. Life Coach vs. Therapist. https://www.tonyrobbins.com/coaching/life-coach-vs-therapist/

- Explore why past relationships (business or personal) have been destructive
- Work through depression or anxiety that affect your ability to function at home or work
- Survive a divorce or loss of a loved one

A COACH, ON THE OTHER HAND, WOULD BE ABLE TO OFFER GUIDANCE BY:

- Clarifying and achieving personal and professional goals
- Creating business plans
- Working to improve communication skills
- Achieving financial independence and security
- Achieving a work/life synergy
- Starting a new business or growing a current business

Investing in coaching has played an integral role in my life, career, and business. While in New York, I learned of an Executive Coach who many of the leaders across our organization had monthly coaching sessions with. I was introduced to her by a peer who was having a great experience with coaching and was one of those work friends that was always looking out for me and speaking my name in rooms I wasn't in. During my journey of deciding how to navigate being in a layoff wave and wanting to take the leap to grow my business, my time with this executive coach was invaluable. Although I wasn't the one making the financial investment with this coach, my sessions with her were invaluable! It opened up my eyes to how critical it is to have a coach when you're working for an organization. To this day, I'm not sure exactly what the rules were for my previous organization in getting an executive coach (I took the "ask for forgiveness instead of permission" approach when I became aware the service was available) but this experience has helped shape the coaching services we offer at Career Thrivers to help emerging leaders gain access to coaching to advance their career! I'm so grateful my company made this investment in me.

Other coaches who guided me through significant life and business shifts were my millionaire business coaches, Jack and Marshawn Daniels. Their mentorship and coaching helped me build my business plan to grow Career Thrivers and exit from my corporate company to become a full-time consultant, speaker, and inclusive leadership coach. In doing so, I've been able to partner with some outstanding organizations to be a strategic partner in cultivating a more inclusive workplace! I've learned so much through investing with Marshawn and Jack to grow my speaking, coaching and consulting business and to upgrade not only my business but especially my mindset and belief!

The Nashville Entrepreneurs Center is a business community, learning and innovation lab, and co-working space that I've leveraged to invest in myself as well. This center offers paid programs that you can invest in to help you grow your business. Shortly after decided to take the severance and leave my organization, I joined a fourteen-week program for founders to build the foundation to test and launch your business. Your city likely has a center or program with resources for business owners. If you're an entrepreneur this may be a great place to seek the support you're looking for.

There are so many I've invested thousands of dollars in my personal and professional development, and I no longer second guess these decisions. These investments in the systems, education, resources, exposure, and network have positioned me to receive the support from others through loss that has accelerated my journey and equipped me to thrive!

STORIES FROM THRIVERS

In addition to investing in support ourselves, we also gain insight and inspiration to help us thrive through from the stories of others. Our experiences that create our stories are really meant to help others thrive through. We've discussed the many different ways grief can present in our lives, from personal to professional loss. Despite grief being a universal emotion that we all experience, it can still be difficult to share the experience with others. Culturally, specifically as Black people, we are conditioned to push through challenges and loss without expressing the fullness of our emotions. To prove we're strong, we suppress our natural emotion of complex, conflicting, and frequently unpredictable feelings in response to a loss or change that disrupts a familiar pattern or prevents the desired outcome. (There's our definition again. ☺) This is why we're on this journey to redefine resilience, and I couldn't think of a better way to take this journey with you than to invite some friends and family to join us!

In addition to sharing many of my losses with you, I thought it would also be beneficial for you to hear the stories of how others thrive through it. I believe it's no accident you're reading this book and that these friends and family members said yes to sharing their story with me to share with you! I'm grateful for their willingness to share their lessons through loss of family, career, opportunities, businesses, and even self. I hope these brief stories will be an inspiration for you on your journey and an invitation for you to share your story as well! Please visit brittanyncole.com/book to share your story with our community! This is how we share the load as we thrive through it, together.

Stephanie Swanigan Gaulmon

MEET STEPHANIE

She and I met at The University of Tennessee, Knoxville (UTK), and she is my prophyte, Soror in Delta, and someone whose grit and grace will inspire you! She's a daughter, sister, wife, senior program manager, and non-profit founder with so much wisdom on how to thrive through the loss of loved ones.

Please share a loss you have experienced.

As a child with adverse childhood experiences, I spent the majority of my childhood with my grandparents. The first significant loss from death was my grandfather in 1986. I was six years old. It was also the first indication that I could supernaturally sense pending unexpected loss. I felt his loss in my gut several days prior to his passing and began to cry when the phone rang, alerting my immediate family. The same occurred with the loss of his wife, my grandmother, in 2008.

My grandmother was a second mother to me with the physical distance between my mother and me. My mother was a full-time musician who traveled 80% of the year and was usually unable to be present for major moments and holidays, so my grandmother filled that void. A few months before she fell ill, I felt the unavoidable urge to drive the 300 miles to see her spontaneously. A few days before her transition, she came to me in a dream. We were sitting in her living room. I could smell the nostalgic aroma of her Sunday dinner. She looked happy and healthy. She told me to prepare for her death.

In 2009, I befriended a local radio personality, and we immediately had a spark. It was more than romantic, so moving in that direction took some time. We were fast friends and bonded over our love of music, Detroit Piston's football, and our love for our transitioned grandmothers. Things turned romantic, and we began to set the foundation to build a future. In 2012, he began to fall into a depression and could not diagnose the cause. One evening while eating dinner at his home and listening to Donny Hathaway's "A Song for You," it was intuitively revealed to me that things were more dire than we thought. I ignored it—this time, no preliminary tears or dreams to alarm me. A few days later, he was gone at only 33 years old. I distinctly remember being told by several people that they admired my grace after such an unexpected and tragic loss. And I wondered if my premonition was really the root of my grace.

In 2016, I met my now-husband. Our relationship started as a friendship as well but quickly progressed to romance. Things became serious when I moved back home to Memphis. I met his family, and he met mine. I adored his father, specifically. We became engaged in 2018. And without any premonition, we lost his father seven months before the wedding. It was unexpected. In the same year, without premonition, we lost our first child two months into pregnancy. We'd experience the deepest loss and joy in the same year.

How would you describe your grief journey through this loss?

I would describe my journey as fluid. I think the premonitions in early loss prepared me to navigate the inevitability of my recent grief. Although certainly not preferable, I think of myself as a grief veteran. It has made me an advocate for mental health and given me a passion for helping others navigate not only grief caused by loss but also grief caused by life.

In what ways did the support of others help you journey forward?

With each loss, the amount of support from others, particularly non-family members, has grown. My decisions to openly share my grief connect me with strangers. It is a universal emotion that binds and ties us as humans.

How did you get comfortable being vulnerable to accept support?

The support of friends and family was the easy part for me. The support and acceptance of professional help were the most difficult. I spent several early sessions in front of therapists who I believe mistook my uncontrollable sobbing as a reason to medicate me. I think a number of them did not have the necessary cultural experience to understand how a college-educated and successful black woman would be so disabled with being vulnerable. Knowing that caused me to hold back, but I knew it did nothing for my progress. After my most recent loss, I knew I had to find someone who I felt comfortable being the most vulnerable with which led me to my active therapist. She has created an environment that makes me feel the most comfortable I have ever felt to freely speak and be vulnerable. It has shifted me in ways where I have clear boundaries on what I share publicly and what I do not.

What advice would you share on how to support someone who is grieving?

Feel all the things. Particularly, black women are conditioned to be strong, with strong being synonymous with soldiering up and not allowing your emotions to bubble up. Not allowing those emotions to breathe will inevitably manifest somewhere else.

Follow Stephanie on Instagram **@iamdefstef**

Vinasia Miles

MEET VINASIA

She and I met at the Black Chamber of Commerce national conference in Washington D.C. and instantly we connected. Vinasia is salt and light and has a passion for serving and lifting others as a daughter, sister, friend, founder, and professor. Check out Vinasia's gems on how to thrive through it below.

Please share a loss you have experienced.

I have experienced loss in quite a few ways, including the death of loved ones, loss of relationships and friendships, loss of intellectual property, job loss, and even the loss of self at times.

How would you describe your grief journey through this loss?

Many prayers and tears, much heartache, and honestly, time with God to seek understanding and peace of mind so that He could lift some of the weight that was holding me down.

In what ways did the support of others help you journey forward?

The encouragement and check-ins from family and friends were helpful. I will forever appreciate those who prayed for and with me.

How did you get comfortable being vulnerable to accept support?

As long as there was established trust, I did not have many issues here. However, it's a process to unlocking vulnerability. That's why I believe having discernment and trust is so important because there will then be a security level for me to be H.O.T (humble, open, and transparent).

What advice would you share on how to support someone who is grieving?

Lean on God through it all. He is the only one that can truly bring you peace, comfort, and understanding. Give yourself grace and time. Understand that it is okay to feel, feel it all, and once you feel, that feeling will become an experience that you'll be able to identify with in the future. Many of the things that we go through or experience are not necessarily for our sake. Yet, we encounter these experiences to be a vessel to help and guide others through the process.

Follow Vinasia on Instagram **@vinasiamile**

Dr. Jessica Williams

MEET JESSICA

We also go back to undergraduate days at UTK. Jessica has always been one to lean into vulnerability and unlock the freedom that comes with living in your truth despite what others say. I love that about her and the way she impacts others as a sister, friend, leadership educator, and wellness advocate. Read her tips on how to thrive through loss and grief below.

Please share a loss you have experienced.

There have been so many! Most notable has been the physical loss of my stepfather and the loss of my former self after an assault.

How would you describe your grief journey through this loss?

It has been ongoing! However, I love the lessons it teaches because I am a hard head and emotional person. Yet, grief is such a palpable feeling. There is no mistaking it, and its command and insistence show me how to surrender and let go.

In what ways did the support of others help you journey forward?

Other people giving me permission to inhabit my feelings fully was the best advice for me. I needed help learning how to stop fighting with grief and to make space for it in my life.

How did you get comfortable being vulnerable to accept support?

Oh, it was 100% forced on me out of necessity, lol! It is hard for me to receive help, but it got to a point to where if I wanted to live, I had to get help.

What advice would you share on how to support someone who is grieving?

Do not hide it. Listen to it and honor it.

Follow Jessica on Instagram **@thejessica_j**

Joshua Mundy

MEET JOSH

You know how you meet people whose positive energy is so contagious it's almost palpable? That's Josh! I don't even know where we met, but he's a serial entrepreneur, speaker, CEO of Pivot Technology School, and "The OG!" Despite a devastating loss to multiple business, check out how Josh has been able to thrive through it.

Please share a loss you have experienced.

On March 3, 2020, a devastating tornado ripped through Tennessee, killing 25 people, injuring more than 300 people, and causing nearly $2 billion in damage. This day truly transformed my life on so many levels. On March 3, gave birth to a new dream and lost three. For twelve years, I built three businesses on the corner of 7th and Jefferson Street in Nashville: Music City Cleaners, theLab, & Events at 624. This corner represented more than just being in business; it was a place that gathered the whole community for decades. It was a place that represented black excellence, and I wanted to carry on that tradition for years to come. This was the place where I saw myself passing down these businesses to my son. But on March 3rd, God had a different plan. On that date, an F4 tornado ripped through 7th and Jefferson, and I saw the dream—the building that housed all three of my businesses— in rubble.

How would you describe your grief journey through this loss?

It was truly a journey, and I saw the divine work of the Lord through it all. I just spent time working on myself and my mental health. Through that experience, I have become a better person and a better businessman.

In what ways did the support of others help you journey forward?

That's really what pushed me through the dark spaces and let me see the light at the end of the tunnel. People really wrapped their arms around my family and me.

How did you get comfortable being vulnerable to accept support?

The worst thing you can do when going through grief is to isolate yourself. A lot of times, people let pride get in the way of seeking wise help and counsel. I have always been a person to share with my closest friends because sometimes grief and loss are too heavy to carry by yourself.

What advice would you share on how to support someone who is grieving?

In the words of Jodeci, "Don't talk just listen!" Sometimes people come in eager to give advice, and sometimes a listening ear is just enough.

Follow Josh on Instagram **@iammrmundy**

Brittainy Hall

MEET BRITTAINY

We met in high school, and she's remained a friend and become a client! Brittainy is a leader and change agent that I've enjoyed getting to watch evolve and thrive! As a believer, daughter, sister, friend, and organizational consultant, Brittany shares how thriving through the death of her best friend has shaped her life.

Please share a loss you have experienced.

In 2005, I lost one of closest childhood friends. We had an amazing friendship of 22 years. We literally watched each other grow up right in front of one another. We had a bond like no other. Amanda meant the world to me, and I miss her presence every day.

How would you describe your grief journey through this loss?

I once read something that described grief like an ocean, and that has never left me. Right when it first happened, the grief felt like I was sitting on the shore where the waves were the strongest. Overtaking me quickly, without a moment's notice. As I journeyed through the process, I started to move deeper into the ocean of grief. Finding that as time went on and the further I moved away from the shore, the calmer things got.

Five years later and deeper in the ocean, the water is a lot calmer, a lot quieter, and at times very still. However, there are those moments when a big wave takes me under, and I become disoriented; but I always manage to resurface. Once I catch my breath and find my bearings, I am then able to coast for a little while longer, ready to face a new wave that will come soon.

In what ways did the support of others help you journey forward?

Being able to talk about my friend, share stories about her, stay connected to her family, and remember the amazing moments we shared has really helped me on this grief journey. It has allowed me to walk through this life with joy in my heart, focusing on all the things that we did share in those 22 years together as friends.

How did you get comfortable being vulnerable to accept support?

I surrendered to the fact that I needed it. Being vulnerable was the only way I was going to make it through.

What advice would you share on how to support someone who is grieving?

Grief is an individualized process, and there is no right or wrong way to grieve. It is your experience. There is no timeline for grief, so allow yourself to feel it. Solicit the support you need and remember finding support in your process isn't a weakness, but yet incredible strength.

Follow Brittainy on Instagram **@victoriapt50**

Verlinda Darden

MEET VERLINDA

She's my best friend, line-sister, and someone I can always count on to be there. Verlinda's resilience throughout her career journey has garnered her several outstanding opportunities to cultivate the economic development of her community and make a positive impact on business leaders, local residents, and community advocates. As a daughter, chief connector, community leader, and external affairs specialist Verlinda will inspire you with how she's been able to thrive through job loss in her career.

Please share a loss you have experienced.

Thirty-three. My Jesus Year, as many call it. To sum it up, it was AN EXPERIENCE— one that truly realigned my career, allowed for self-examination, shifted my perspective and priorities, and catapulted me into my destiny.

How would you describe your grief journey through this loss?

Anyone who knows me knows I'm pretty calculated in my moves. I seek opportunities that prove beneficial and generally have a positive impact. Welp, *inserts laugh* to say my last career opportunity didn't fit the mold would sell God's Plan short of its intended outcome for my life. I thought I had reached the pinnacle of my career. I worked for one of the nation's most renowned government entities and was doing the work I loved, community and workforce development. As I was continually building my foundation and making a name for myself in the industry impacting lives, the grounding below me quickly collapsed. I'm not sure if you have ever experienced job loss when things seem to be going well, but I wouldn't wish this on my worst enemy. It is truly a time of fight or flight. One filled with emotion, grit, grind, and let me not forget much prayer. My good friend, Isaac Addae once wrote, "When battling giants in your life, find a way to live above what you're facing, lean on your faith, and never lose sight of the greatness within you." Those are wise words to live by. I won't say it is a journey in which you won't grow weary, but you must believe and have faith in God's promises for your life, Jeremiah 29:11. Maintaining confidence in Him will bless you and help you move forward when you can't see the stairwell or its ending. Continuously speaking of God's love and promise, an amazing support system, and my professional network helped me make it through to the other side. I am now experiencing some of the best days of my life, a greater opportunity, and look forward to what's to come. "It keeps happening for me," and I'm thankful. Thank You, Lord.

In what ways did the support of others help you journey forward?

God, my circle and professional network are AMAZING! Each helped me to move through my journey gracefully. God is so faithful and keeps his promises. He just kept blowing my mind throughout the entire process. My circle is second to none, and I feel blessed to have the unwavering love and support of friends, family, and acquaintances who push me to be my greatest self.

How did you get comfortable being vulnerable to accept support?

Wow. This took some time. I believe when you're viewed as someone who "has it together," you feel you have no room for error. So when job loss happens, whether you're at fault or a casualty to organizational restructuring, you tend to feel like you've failed and can't ask for help. It's a crippling feeling and a major blow. So telling my close circle was hard, and reaching out to my professional network was even harder. I didn't want to answer any questions, and at the beginning, I was resentful of the organization. Yet working through my feelings and realizing I couldn't do it alone helped me come to terms with it and proved beneficial in the end.

What advice would you share on how to support someone who is grieving?

Be there for the person and don't insert yourself or personalize the experience. Be a sounding board. Remind them of their greatness and resiliency, and most of all, BE A GOOD HUMAN. We could all use one in our time of need. Lastly, don't forget to be yourself. People value authenticity and can see when it's a genuine act of concern. Let's be a light for each other.

Follow Verlinda on Instagram **@verli.d**

Dr. Bryan Johnson

MEET BRYAN

He's my brother and one of the best leaders I know! He's always been a servant leader, as I have many memories of him agreeing to help me clean my room and straighten out the clothes in my closet growing up! Three days after our mom died I witnessed God's strength in his weakness and Bryan's resilience as he travelled to Chattanooga, TN to interview for the Superintendent of Schools position. He's been serving in that capacity since and has lead Hamilton County to pivot and reach historic results in student academic growth! My brother is one of four finalist for Superintendent of the Year for 2020, and I believe he's going to win!

Please share a loss you have experienced.

The death of my mother.

How would you describe your grief journey through this loss?

It's taken a lot of prayer and belief that God's plans are always perfect. As scripture teaches, His ways aren't our ways and His thoughts aren't our thoughts. My wife, Candy, and my family have been key in my journey. What I found even more challenging has been watching my father navigate the loss.

In what ways did the support of others help you journey forward?

My wife and family have been a major source of support. Having family to talk to and pray with has been helpful throughout this journey. Additionally spending time with God has made all the difference. Praying and spending time in God's word has helped me through hard days and tough moments.

How did you get comfortable being vulnerable to accept support?

The realization that I couldn't handle the grief alone helped me open up. It was a challenge as I often internalize my thoughts and feelings, but I had to learn to become comfortable with being vulnerable.

What advice would you share on how to support someone who is grieving?

Trust God and receive the support from family and friends. Remember the good times spent and all that your loved one gave you. This is truly the gift.

Follow Bryan on **LinkedIn Bryan Johnson Ed.D.**

It is my hope that this chapter and these stories have inspired you to support others through loss whether you're a family member, friend, colleague, or ally. I also hope it has shed some light on how to embrace vulnerability to share the load whether you share with a friend, coach, or therapist. Whoever is in your pyramid of support, there is one common denominator – the transformation you want to see requires you to show up and share! Now it's your turn; how will you share the load?

Thoughts along the journey:

8. Share The Load

1. How have you shared your story to share the load?

2. What is keeping you from being vulnerable and receiving grace?

3. Name one person to begin to be vulnerable with to share exactly where you are right now.

4. How can that person continue to support you?

5. What coaching or therapy resources are available to assist you?

CHAPTER 9

Proceed with Grace

I'm not moving on; I'm thriving through

Thriving is first a mindset. Before what we envision can be seen, we must first believe it's possible. It's natural to have questions around how the vision will manifest. How will this be possible? How can I get through this? How will I make it? Why did this have to happen? What am I going to do? I want to encourage you. Despite having more questions than answers and having your plans shredded in a matter of moments—keep believing, keep being, and keep building. You are enough, and you have enough to get through this. Everything you need is within you. The people who are meant to support you to help you build your next normal will find you. You may be down due to change and loss, but you aren't out. I'm rooting for you. Here are some affirmations to help you thrive through.

> *You are enough, and you have enough to get through this. Everything you need is within you. The people who are meant to support you to help you build your next normal will find you.*

AFFIRMATIONS FOR PROCEEDING WITH GRACE

I am equipped to thrive through my current challenges. Everything I need is within me. Obstacles are opportunities to reimagine and recreate in unprecedented ways. I'm a thriver!

Self-care is service. Today I will make time to be present to give myself what I need today to thrive.

I thrive under pressure and also know how to use my voice and boundaries to prevent burnout. If I need help, I will ask. If I'm uncomfortable, I will speak up. I am granting myself grace and have everything I need to thrive through this season.

Today I will decide to see all the good around me—even if I have to squint. I am right where I'm meant to be and will learn something new today.

Every experience is an opportunity for continuous improvement. I'm prepared and ready to learn, grow, and improve. I am proud of my progress.

I am resilient. Resilience isn't just about my ability to push through; it's also about being brave enough to be honest, and transparent with someone else about where I've been, where I am, and where I'm going. Today I will share my story with someone else to encourage them to keep thriving!

I am becoming. I will hold myself to challenging but realistic expectations of what I can achieve today. I will celebrate each goal I accomplish with gratitude and joy. Every decision I make brings me closer to my goal and the best version of myself.

My career is a marathon, not a sprint. Challenges will come. I may fumble, but I will not fold under pressure. I am resilient.

Joy isn't a result of my circumstances. It is my constant state of mind. Today I will find joy in simple pleasures.

My setbacks are a setup for innovation, creativity, and grace. Today I will trust myself and try something new even if it feels strange.

Growth happens beyond my comfort zone. If I'm not stretched or challenged somehow, I will find an opportunity to get uncomfortable.

I will keep calm and maintain my peace of mind in challenging situations today. I was built for this!

I protect my energy by making having a positive perspective a priority. Today I choose to radiate positive energy that will impact those around me to keep thriving.

I am engaged in creating an inclusive workplace where my colleagues and I feel we belong. I will speak up and model tactful correction if inappropriate conversations arise so we can all proceed with grace.

I am patient with myself and with those around me. I cultivate strategic, valuable, and positive relationships that bring out the best in me.

DAILY WORK & FORGIVENESS

As you journey through your next normal, whether it is a new career opportunity, a new relationship, a new routine, or the new absence of someone you can no longer call or see, it is essential to remember to give yourself grace. This is daily work. You will toggle between grief and gratitude, anger and appreciation, confusion, and confidence. This is natural. It's part of the work, and the work is about daily progress, even if it's maintaining the progress you made the day before.

> *Give yourself grace. This is daily work. You will toggle between grief and gratitude, anger and appreciation, confusion, and confidence.*

Part of the progress that helps us journey through is recognizing the need for forgiveness along the way. We must understand that forgiveness releases us from the anger and resentment we may naturally feel due to adversity. Harboring unforgiveness in our hearts holds us hostage to staying in that place. Forgiveness is not about the person that committed the offense, but

> *Part of the progress that helps us journey through is recognizing the need for forgiveness along the way.*

forgiveness is about you. Forgiveness is you. Forgiveness is defined as ceasing to feel resentment against an offender. When we release those feelings of resentment and forgive, we release the control the person or circumstance has on our lives. If we're going to thrive through the change, challenge, and loss in our lives, forgiveness of ourselves and others is part of the journey.

When I experienced that moment of forgiveness for myself with Thasunda on her Instagram Live event, I also realized I had to forgive my mom. Not only did I grieve her death, but I was also angry with her. I know now there were things her doctors shared with her and my dad and kept from me. My mom was always like this, private and protective. She wanted nothing but the best for my brothers and me—even if that meant keeping the worst from us. Although I disagreed with her philosophy on this growing up, I understand it. In those fragile and final weeks in May of 2017, she chose to prioritize my new career opportunity in New York and newly stable living conditions with my husband, over sharing every detail of her prognosis. This angered me. I didn't understand why she would keep these details from me that would've entirely changed my decisions leading up to her death. I certainly would've come home had I known all she knew. Or maybe she knew more but was struggling to believe all she had been told. Maybe her faith wouldn't let her repeat the prognosis. She had beaten so many negative reports before with her congestive heart failure, so maybe her faith wouldn't allow her to share what she didn't believe. Either way, this is where I've learned the sovereignty of God in new ways. There was and is nothing I can do to change those moments that God allowed and the ones He didn't allow. I've had to learn to trust how even these finite and final details were in His control. Therefore, I had to forgive her. This is the only way to heal fully, take a breath, and forgive yourself… and them.

Forgiveness is hard, but it can be easier when you forgive someone you love. What happens when the offender has zero influence on you, and you don't have to interact with them? You must still forgive to deal and heal.

FORGIVENESS AND FORTITUDE AT YOUR 9-5

As Maya Angelou said, "When people show you who they are, believe them the first time, "even when they look like you. As I shared with you, I led a sales team in 2019 while also being in a layoff wave and looking for other opportunities. There were options, but all of the ones presently available seemed meh. I was hopeful other opportunities would present themselves as the company was relatively early in the organizational change process. I also couldn't sit around and let things happen to me when there were opportunities to create the life I wanted. Throughout the layoffs across the company, it was clear the already low percentage of Black colleagues were taking a hit. There was a maddingly obvious need for inclusion and equity across the organization, and there was a recent diversity, equity, and inclusion (DEI) global leader hired to build out a team and meet it. We were well acquainted as I was leading several initiatives across our Black and women ERGs. Despite leading these impactful programs and initiatives, it was clear they were just that—short term and not sustainable based on the structure we had. So, I decided to propose an alternative. It was clear we needed a DEI leader within the business—the sales organization specifically. I got insight from leaders on responsibilities to include in pitching this role. Some of the priorities this person would be responsible for included an ERG strategy that was aligned to the DEI strategy and goals, implementation to reduce duplication, and serving as a liaison to the Global DEI team to mobilize, support, and train sales leaders. Typically, DEI sits within legal and HR and can be very compliance focused. The data is clear that if companies want to cultivate an inclusive culture, then the entire organization from human resources to the business leaders to middle management must be actively engaged in the work.[17]

I put together a plan and cleared it with my leadership to connect with key stakeholders across the business, ERGs, and HR for feedback and alignment. The goal of these meetings was to uncover aspects of the recommendation that wouldn't work and gain insight on what to add or adjust. Once I got the green light, I hit the ground running. Nearly every leader I spoke with was supportive and impressed. More importantly, they were in overwhelming agreement that this was a problem that needed to be addressed and the solution I was recommending – although innovative for our organization – made sense. I also received new insight on the depth of the problem and additional responsibilities that could be added to this role. Throughout my conversations with senior leaders, it was clear that if approved this role could seamlessly proceed as a pilot. Piloting new roles as interim short-term projects was not new at all; however, taking a strategic approach to diversity, equity, and inclusion inside the business hadn't been done in this way before.

Most of the leaders were aligned and excited about this possibility except for a handful of colleagues. This was to be expected. Certainly, I didn't except everyone to be on board. However I also didn't expect that most of the resistance I was receiving would come from

---

[17] Juliet Bourke and Bernadette Dillon. The Diversity and Inclusion Revolution. Deloitte Review. Issue 22, January 2018.

colleagues that looked like me. One colleague was so bothered by the entire process that she yelled at me on a call and wanted an apology about how the stakeholder alignment meetings had progressed. At the time I couldn't believe the toxic behavior coming from this senior Black leader directed at me for sharing a proposal for a problem that she saw clearly and worked to solve every day.

Shortly after my exchange with her, the senior leader that would make the final decision went from sharing how much the role was needed and the potential for an interim role (similar to the one I was in at the time) to a complete about face in tone and interest in proceeding with the proposed role. Although several components of the proposal ended up being implemented, the plan was declined. Shortly after, I was approached to do "something similar" as a new diversity recruiter. As it turned out, the role wasn't diversity recruiting, and everyone was confused about what I would be doing, including me. It became quite clear that the pull I felt to be and do more was actually meant to happen beyond the organization I was apart of.

Leave the door open and keep the ladder down is a saying from pioneer of corporate diversity programs Bernard Kinsey who in the 1970s helped to make Xerox a more inclusive workplace. This was more than a saying for Black colleagues at Xerox; it became a code of ethics for how they championed each other. As we work together to channel our fortitude to make the workplace work for everyone and challenge non-BIPOC colleagues to speak up, step up, and walk the talk of allyship, I'd be remiss not to share this reminder to leave the door open and the ladder down. Black trauma in predominantly white workplaces isn't always at the hands of white people. Workplace trauma of Black professionals by other Black professionals can be the most traumatic of all.

Despite feeling frustrated about the resistance, I experienced I felt so sure that what was proposed was needed that I was grateful to have the opportunity to have these conversations with so many leaders. Despite the sting of disrespect from another Black woman in the workplace where we were few, I knew I had to forgive her and move on. I also knew that there was purpose in what I thought was an ideal opportunity not working. I live by the motto that every experience is an opportunity for continuous improvement. My dad would always tell my brothers and I growing up that, "The biggest room in our house is the room for improvement!" Throughout this entire experience were lessons to learn from and opportunities for me to improve. Staying was the safe path, and I thought I would be able to create an opportunity to serve in an expansive way like I'd had so many times before. But I also couldn't deny this pull that there was more – more to be, more to do, and more impact to make. I decided not to pursue another internal role and took the leap to grow my speaking, coaching, and consulting business full-time. I rebranded my company to Career Thrivers in 2019, and growing our inclusive leadership development firm been one of the best decisions I've ever made! Being able to partner with organizations to cultivate a culture where everyone believes they belong is an absolute joy!

FEEL THE LOSS. FOCUS FORWARD

Change, challenge, and loss often reveal our most authentic priorities and purpose. Through the challenge of not taking a job everyone thought I should, losing a parent while working, and even being laid off from Pfizer after nearly twelve years, I've cemented my priorities and clarified my purpose. Yes, this is part of thriving through loss. In tandem, I've also had to keep my focus forward.

Feeling the pain and focusing forward helps us to stay grateful for all things. Let's revisit Hebrews 12:2. These verses teach us how to be consistent in our resilience through our faith and our focus. Verse 2 says, "We do this [lay aside the weights that slow us down and run the race set before us] by keeping our eyes on Jesus, the champion who initiates and perfects our faith. Because of the joy awaiting him, he endured the cross, disregarding its shame. Now he is seated in the place of honor beside God's throne" (NLT). I get excited every time I read this verse! Jesus endured the pain of the cross by focusing on the joy that was set before Him. He had a vision of what would be through the present pain, and that helped Him endure. What is the joy that is set before you? Where is your focus? Are you looking at the pain, or are you focused on the promise in front of you? When we have a vision of where we're going and who we're meant to become, this becomes the focus and force that pulls us up and forward.

As we focus and move forward in faith, we will see ourselves in the fullness of who we are. It's in moments of change, challenge, and loss we come into a more profound revelation of who we're meant to become. There is a level of divine strength I didn't know existed prior to the losses in my life. These hardships have proven to help me grow in amazing ways I never knew before or that I was capable of. In addition to seeing myself more clearly, loss has also helped me to see others and their intention for being part of my life more clearly. Seasons of adversity show you who is genuinely for you. The fickle friends and colleagues will flee immediately, and your true circle will reveal themselves. I'll never forget the words of someone I thought was a mentor until I turned down the Viagra role. He told me I had "committed career suicide." I was shocked and hurt by his words. I was also so incredibly grateful to see him more clearly during that loss in my career.

Those challenging moments show you who believes in you, who sees you beyond the choices you make, and who supports who you are and not just what you can do for them. There will be those who leave your life as you thrive through adversity, and there will be others who show up and stand up in their place. It may seem like your circle is getting smaller when you're met with the change, challenge, and loss, but in actuality, it's getting stronger. It's like the difference between fat and muscle; muscle takes up less space, but it's heavier, leaner, and will carry you further.

> *Those challenging moments show you who believes in you, who sees you beyond the choices you make, and who supports who you are and not just what you can do for them.*

Now that you are more precise on your purpose, setting boundaries around your priorities, and investing in the people who value you more than your gifts and talents, it's time to journey forward. I can tell you that the journey forward looks different for each of us. This book was never intended to be a one-size-fits-all approach. The Resilience Roadmap® is a guide. The experience throughout the journey is up to you. These are not linear step processes you need to go through, and these certainly are not tips you need to check off a list. However, think of each of these rest stops as a marker of your progress.

As you decide how to proceed with grace through the change, challenge, and loss, commit to the process. It can be very easy, especially after a traumatic loss, to throw yourself back into your work or parenthood or whatever it is to distract you from the pain you feel. Yes, it's important to settle into a routine and attend to your responsibilities. I also hope I've encouraged you to be mindful and intentional to give yourself what you need to address the difficult feelings, spiraling thoughts, and hard conversations. Helping to make people and processes better come naturally to me. For some time, I leaned on everyone else's need of me to keep me busy, so I didn't have to deal with myself to heal. What does it look like to journey through and forward?

> *As you decide how to proceed with grace through the change, challenge, and loss, commit to the process.*

HOW TO PROCEED WITH GRACE

By now, you know how much I love acronyms and acrostics and use them as a way to retain information. Here is our next to last one that will help you to **proceed with G.R.A.C.E.** as you thrive through it!

GRATITUDE – Give yourself grace through gratitude. Begin and end your day with gratitude. This practice has helped me get through days when I wasn't sure if I'd see the next one. Having a consistent prayer practice to express gratitude and praise has helped me learn to live a life of gratitude. Philippians 4:6–7 is one of my favorite reminders of the power of being thankful. "Be anxious for nothing but in everything by prayer and supplication with thanksgiving let your requests be made known to God; and the peace of God, which surpasses all understanding, will guard your hearts and your minds through Jesus Christ" (NKJV). Another way to practice gratitude is to utilize affirmations to manage your mindset and maintain a growth mindset of gratitude and abundance.

REST – Give yourself grace through rest. Our bodies, minds, and spirits need rest to be **R.estored, E.fficient, S.trengthened, and T.houghtful.** Okay, you got me! It's another acronym I squeezed in here. Rest is critical for thriving through.

Furthermore, remember those benefits of rest when you're considering whether to work seven days a week or take a day to rest and recalibrate. When you choose to rest, you're giving yourself the grace to be Restored, Efficient, Strengthened, and Thoughtful. As a result, you end up being much more productive and proficient when you make time to rest.

> *When you choose to rest, you're giving yourself the grace to be restored, efficient, strengthened, and thoughtful.*

ACCEPTANCE – Give yourself grace through acceptance. This one can be tough, but you will get there as you navigate the Resilience Roadmap ®. Often the acceptance we need comes through those Empathy Conversations. Even if you don't have every single question answered, you will get to a point where you live out the Serenity Prayer to "accept the things you cannot change, the courage to change the things you can, and the wisdom to know the difference." If you're a believer, continue to pray and ask God to grant you wisdom and peace to accept what you cannot change.

CONFIDENCE – Give yourself grace through confidence. As an inclusive leadership and career branding coach, this is one of the most significant outcomes my clients express they've gained during our time together. This always catches my attention because it's rarely a challenge they express initially in the process. What am I saying? Our confidence can slip so subtly we don't even realize we're second-guessing ourselves and doubting every decision we make. Often it isn't that we don't know what to do. We lack the confidence to make the decision we know we need to make for ourselves and others. Consider journaling as a way to express your feelings and get to the source of any areas where you lack confidence. Don't think of journaling as this gigantic writing exercise taking lots of time. It doesn't. Journaling can be as simple as spending 5–10 minutes before bed getting your thoughts down on paper. There's no blueprint for this. You don't have to write it in a specific format. You don't have to worry about being grammatically correct. You can just write your thoughts in an honest, transparent, and non-judgmental way. Through loss, I found it helpful to journal my thoughts and feelings to acknowledge them and build my confidence in areas I noticed were struggles for me.

Another way to boost our confidence is to seek out resources, tools, and support to learn what we don't know. Competence breeds confidence. By investing in developing my skills and investing in coaching and therapy, I saw my confidence increase. Perhaps for you, proceeding with grace involves going beyond "researching" a therapist and making a decision on one, and booking the appointment. Whatever it looks like for you, step out of your comfort zone to make an investment in yourself that will lead to an increase in your confidence.

> *Competence breeds confidence.*

EMPATHY – Give others grace through empathy. As you're proceeding with grace, I can guarantee you that others will need it as well. You will inevitably have moments of, "Did they say that?" or "Why don't they know that already?" Remember what we discussed about Empathy Conversations and extend grace to others as you journey forward to thrive through. How you respond and even share your journey through change, challenge, and loss could be a teachable moment for them to enable a transformational shift for everyone involved.

Well, there you have it! You've successfully walked through **The Resilience Roadmap** ® and know where to go for future reference as you redefine resilience in your life to thrive through with courage, purpose, and joy! To access your Thrive Through It toolkit, remember to visit brittanyncole.com/book.

Thoughts along the journey:

9. Focus Forward

In the space below, write a letter to your future self. Imagine you are three years removed from this moment. It may be hard to see farther than that when you're hurting. What would you say to yourself in three years? What lessons have you learned? What have you overcome? What are you proud of? What goals have you achieved? What does work look like? What does your family look like?

Write a letter to future _____.

_____
_____
_____
_____
_____
_____
_____
_____
_____

CHAPTER 10

Gratitude

"You can be sad, angry, frustrated, and grateful."

Together, we are redefining resilience to thrive through whatever obstacle we face with courage, authenticity, purpose, and joy. When we're experiencing hard moments, it is easy to wish them away. Towards the end of a hard year such as 2020, we're all waiting and ready to "hurry up" and get over it so we can celebrate what's next. I can relate to this as 2017 was that year for me, and if I was sharing a cliff notes version of the journey it would be:

2017 was a year of extremes. I'd accomplished a big career goal and learned through experience what resilience and persistence truly meant when it came to advancing my career. I worked hard to change those perceptions and get that marketing role, again. Talk about a high! My husband and I moved to my dream city so I could take on my new marketing role—one that no one had had before, and I just knew was meant for me!

Enter disruption.

Three months after relocating from Chattanooga to New York my mom's health unexpectedly declined and she died. My world suddenly stopped and seemingly shattered right before my eyes. My heart was broken into a million pieces that one day may mend but will never fit back the same way again. 2017 brought a whole new meaning to the word resilience and the amazing power of belief. I was so glad to welcome the new year.

The fact of the matter was when I sat down to journey through the Resilience Roadmap® at the end of 2017, just as you have in this book, I had so much to be grateful for. I was clearer on my purpose and priorities than I had ever been. I had amazing colleagues whose kindness, unknowingly to them, carried me through that year. I had a husband who was supportive and committed to walking with me through my lowest moments. I even had, what I didn't know then would be, the beginning of a best-selling book that would transform the lives of people just like you to thrive through it!

I didn't see all of this initially. However, as I stopped trying to get over the deepest pain I've experienced and leaned in to journey through it, there was so much to learn from and be grateful for. When we rush to show up as who we aren't yet, it can lead to toxic positivity that perpetuates a cycle of wearing a cape and a mask to hide where we are. You don't have to act happy if you really aren't.

TOXIC POSITIVITY

Many of us are living in a perpetual state of toxic positivity, and I hope the Resilience Roadmap® helps us course correct. Toxic positivity is the excessive overgeneralization of a happy or optimistic state that often results in the denial, minimization, and invalidation of our natural, authentic human emotional experience. We can actually use optimism as a cover to silence our human experience. This happens often with grief, and it is toxic indeed. I want to help us get FREE so we can stop pretending and just be. This is critical because toxic positivity leads to isolation, stress, depression, shame and other mental and emotional challenges. According to a study in the Journal of Abnormal Psychology by Drs. James Gross and Robert Levenson titled Hiding Feelings: The Acute Effects of Inhibiting Negative and Positive Emotion they share that hiding one's emotion as a route to alleviate negative feelings can actually lead to more stress![18]

> *We can actually use optimism as a cover to silence our human experience. I want to help us get FREE so we can stop pretending and just be.*

Here are some signs to help you recognize how toxic positivity shows up:

- Feeling you have to hide your true feelings
- Feeling guilty for how you feel
- Minimizing or dismissing the feelings of others with quotes or Scripture
- Rationalizing the feelings of others to share a logical or comparative perspective

---

[18] James J. Gross and Robert W. Levenson. Hiding Feelings: The Acute Effects of Inhibiting Negative and Positive Emotion. The Journal of Abnormal Psychology, 1997.

Here are some examples of statements from The Psychology Group to shift our language to be more accepting and validating:

TOXIC POSITIVITY	NON-TOXIC ACCEPTANCE
"Everything happens for a reason."	"Sometimes we can draw the short straw in life. How can I support you during this difficult time?"
"Everything will work out in the end"	"This is really hard. I'm thinking of you."
"Don't think about it, stay positive!"	"Describe what you're feeling. I'm listening."
"Positive vibes only!"	"I'm here for you, both good and bad."
"If I can do it, so can you!"	"Everyone's story, abilities and boundaries are different and that's okay."
"Don't worry, be happy!"	"It seems like you're stressed. What can I help you with?"
"Failure is not an option."	"Failure is a part of growth and success."
"Look for the silver lining."	"I see you. I'm here for you."
"It could be worse."	"That's terrible. I'm so sorry you're going through this."
"Don't look at the negative."	"Suffering is a part of life, and you are not alone."

DON'T PRETEND TO BE POSITIVE. BE FREE

In the midst of my "get over it" year in 2017, I wrote a blog post that I want to share with you here:

I'm Not OK and That's OKAY!

"How are you doing?"

It's one of the most common questions asked of people who care about you. I am always appreciative when people are kind enough to ask about me. It suggests a level of selflessness and concern that people don't have to express. These calls and messages of kindness are also a source of strength when going through hard times. However, do you ever find yourself, despite circumstances, giving the automatic and trained response of affirmative wellbeing instead of your actual, transparent present truth?

"I'm fine... good... doing pretty good..."

Instead of

"I'm NOT good... terrible... hurting beyond description... angry... at the breaking point..."

This is rarely ever my response. Instead, I will myself to give the most positive answer I can, "blessed and highly favored" knowing good and well I'm really "broken and hardly functioning." Why do we do this?

Candidly, I simply don't want to share negative energy. Even if it means masking my mood, I want others to feel better in my presence than they did before they came. Bottom line, I want to be positive. But when we take this approach time and time again, are we really holding ourselves to an unrealistic standard that even Christ didn't set for Himself? What was the image of Christ in moments when He was in pain?

My mind keeps going back to Jesus at the cross. One of the countless things I love about the Lord is that in all His sovereignty, He was still fully human and completely related to our natural emotional responses of anger, sadness, questioning and even pain. The beauty of the cross, especially at this point of my life, is that Jesus didn't pretend not to feel.

As many times as I've heard and even taught on Jesus' Seven Last Sayings on the cross, I realize at times I missed the mere humanity in His experience. The anguish of Jesus' physical and spiritual pain in His suffering and separation is evident at the cross, and if Jesus in all of His omnipotence can express His pain and suffering why is it that we that are in the body of Christ are always so quick to mask ours?

I believe that the lack of transparency within the church (body of believers) to honestly express our weaknesses prevents healing and hinders discipleship. Here is what I am continuing to learn each day in this season of sometimes unbearable pain.

In order to heal and be F.R.E.E.:

1. We need to FEEL

It's impossible to work towards healing if we don't allow ourselves to fully feel. The awareness of our emotion is essential to knowing how to properly handle it. Masking what we feel—for the pseudo benefit of ourselves or others—doesn't prevent the feeling, it just postpones the improper management of it. Be free to allow yourself to be present in your pain, weakness, sadness, hurt and anger. The more we hide how we feel, the more those same feelings grow.

Feeling is the first step to healing.

2. We need to RELATE

This one is going to get a little tight, and I share this with the upmost appreciation, honesty, and respect. Sometimes, in moments when people are going through, they don't always need a theological exegesis of how they should be responding. (Hello, emotional intelligence!) Okay, so hear me out… I. LOVE. THE. LORD! I really, truly do. I love His Word. It's in my heart. It refreshes me. It lifts me. It is my true foundation. AND YET…There are times when relationship is truly needed over religion. When "I'm here for you… I feel your pain… I've been there… " are necessary bridges to Romans 8:28. I truly believe this is the essence of salt and light and the true message of Jesus Christ, relating to people right where they are and loving them to The Truth of God's Word.

3. We need to EXPRESS

We can't heal what we don't reveal. Whether it is writing, talking, praying, dancing, therapy, mentorship or a combination of all six, it is so vital to our healing to outwardly express what we feel. The relating aspect can help to facilitate expressing what we feel in a way that is productive to our healing.

4. Finally, we need to EXCHANGE

Once we feel, relate and express then we position ourselves to make the exchange. Sometimes I believe we enter this step prematurely and exchange our feelings for things that make us worse off. However, I would submit to you that God is able to exchange our tears for joy and gratitude. If we are prayerful throughout our process and persist in His presence in the midst of our pain, He is faithful to truly give peace that surpasses our ability to put into words.

It's okay to not be okay, but please be FREE!

Most days at some point in the day I am NOT okay. Grief is so unpredictable. I can be having a good moment and a certain smell, place or thought will trigger a memory that sends me into an emotional wreck. My only strength is the Holy Spirit reminding me in those moments of what I know, and the only way back to being okay is to be FREE and allow Him to exchange my weakness for His strength!

BE WELL

Thank you for taking the time to redefine resilience with me! I hope this book helped to shift your perspective on grief, loss, resilience, and more. My hope and prayer is that you will continue to reflect and reference this book as a resource on your resilience journey and continue to **BE WELL:**

B – BELIEVE BEYOND WHERE YOU ARE

Acknowledge the truth of where you are today and continue to believe beyond your present experience. What do you believe?

E – ENCOURAGE YOURSELF DAILY

Develop a rhythm of speaking life to and about yourself. Our words create our world.

W – WRITE DOWN WHERE YOU WANT TO BE

Even if journaling and writing isn't your thing, at the very least write down the vision you have of the life and business you want. Who do you want to become? Write that down.

E – EXERCISE YOUR BODY

Get moving. Movement helped me through 2017 – walking to or from work in New York and taking a stroll through Central Park on the weekends helped me thrive through. Sometimes we have to move our body first to help our minds move.

L – LOOK FOR THE LESSON

Every experience is an opportunity for continuous improvement. If you're experiencing it, there's a lesson in it. Look for it.

L – LET YOUR GUARD DOWN

Vulnerability is courage, and sometimes you just have to leap into it.

You are a thriver, and I am rooting for you! Be well and let's thrive, together!

SIX LOVE LETTERS
to my
M.O.T.H.E.R.

In May of 2017 for Mothers Day, one month before my mother's death, I was living in New York and wanted to do something really special for her that I couldn't order or purchase. I decided to write her letters the week leading up to Mothers Day and send them to her. At her funeral on June 10, 2017 I printed the letters in a booklet and shared them with our family and friends. These lessons she taught me are part of her legacy, and I want to share them with you.

BRITTANY N. COLE THRIVE THROUGH IT

June 10, 2017

Dear friends and family,

Thank you so much for your presence today.

In the days leading up to this past Mother's Day, I knew I wanted to do something for my mom that she would enjoy, and God placed on my heart to share the life lessons that she's taught me in letters.

I'd already purchased my ticket to be home for Mother's Day, but because we live in New York now, I knew it would take too long to put them in the mail each day. I wanted her to see them in the days leading up to Mother's Day, so I wrote them out on my blog, and each day, I would send her the link of the letter with one of my favorite pictures of us. When we talked on the phone about them, I told her I would print them out in a booklet for her to keep.

There are so many things that my mom taught me about life, family, career, friendship, womanhood, and most of all, living for the Lord. I hope that these lessons will be a blessing to you as they are to me. She was truly my very best friend, and I will try my very best to live these lessons and make her proud.

Love,

Brittany N. Cole

M – Mission and Marriage

Dear Mom –

Of all the flowers I can give you the most fragrant petals I'll always have to share are the lessons I've learned because of the life you've lived. My prayer is that these six days leading up to Mother's Day will be days of strength, smiles, peace, and mirroring back to you all of the love you've poured out in overflow. We – Bryan, Troy, Daddy, and I are forever grateful for the matriarch of love that you are.

Over the next six days, I want to share with you six truths you've taught me and just say thank you! I honor you and love you so much! I thank God that I have the privilege of proximity to know that your life – every day – replicates the commitment to Christ you taught us to have. Your mission and measure are always the Master.

My Wedding Day

These two life lessons – mission & marriage – are probably the most important seeds you've sown in me as a woman. Your most important mission has always been walking in faith to glorify God and edify His people. Some talk about their mission. Nowadays, we post our mission and find creative ways to display it. The lesson I've learned from your life is the power in living your mission. Your faith in Christ inspires me, and so many others. Beyond your profession of faith, I've watched your persistence to live a life of faith. Your belief in God has carried you through a life of caring for others, sacrificing convenience for the sake of service, always supporting daddy's call to pastoring when it would've been entirely understandable to miss meetings and multiple services, ensuring we always had the best even if it meant you worked in less-than-ideal conditions. I'm not sure I'd be able to say I know what a woman of faith tangibly looks like if it hadn't been for how you are walking through this life – despite the losses and challenges. Man will always have a say in who you should be, what you should do, advice you should take, but you've always made your measure in life the Master of life. If He says it, that settles it for you, and if He hasn't, good luck trying to convince you! Lol! I love your steadfast, unmovable spirit – most of the time. ☺

The other lesson I've been keenly aware of over the last few years is a woman's place in marriage. I'm not sure I've ever been challenged more in my life; there are aspects of this marriage walk that you don't know and can't even begin to speak on until you're in it. I've watched from your example that even your marriage is linked to and fueled by your mission. Regardless of what you may think in a moment about daddy, the covenant is with Christ, and that keeps you committed. Faith undergirds your feelings, and you keep moving forward. How in the world do people do marriage without Christ!? I've watched how you support daddy, love him, and strengthen him to lead our family. It encourages me to do the same with Joe, to look beyond what I see in the present sometimes, and have faith in the covenant I made that God will strengthen the weakness and stand in the gap. People aren't honest and transparent about marriage. Still, I'm grateful that you and daddy have always kept it 100 (that means really honest lol) about the work that marriage is and how it will only be as fruitful as our commitment to each other and covenant with Christ, keeping Him at the center.

Thank you for being such a wonderful mother to me – STYLE and Substance personified! You are THE BEST! I love you and look forward to writing to you tomorrow.

O – Order & Obedience

Tuesday, May 10, 2017

Dear Mom –
"Let all things be done decently and in order." 1 Corinthians 14:40

Pastoral Anniversary

You made sure we knew this verse; I thought it was your quote until I finally realized it's a Bible verse, lol!

I appreciate you teaching me that getting things done is only part of the task; the true effort is to get things done. You've shown me that there is an order to faith, family, finances, and even friendships.

"Get a good education, work, and make a good living for yourself, see the world, get married, see the world, have some babies..." You and daddy have shared some version of this order my entire life. There have been plenty of times that I've been out of order, but as a young woman, this lesson has always echoed in the back of my mind. There is a divine order to life and building a family intended to produce a smoother transition from 2 becoming one and then multiplying. At the same time, you taught me compassion and humility, not looking down on those that reversed the family order, and not to think highly of myself in pursuit of proper order.

Sometimes it's hard to pursue proper order because we aren't obedient to God's way of living life. Jesus is explicit in His teachings on faith, family, finances, and friendships, and when to submit to His way and are obedient to His word, the order of life becomes easy.

You've been a young professional moving from Charleston to Tennessee to pursue your career, a wife that made a new life in Nashville with daddy, a working mom balancing raising us and supporting others as a social worker, an at-home mom attentive to our adolescent changing years and a best friend as you've supported me in establishing my own order of life as an adult.

I appreciate your example of obedience and order to remain steadfast in prioritizing your faith and family, wise in the stewardship of your finances, and selfless and supportive in your friendships.
I love you and know you're up late, so I hope you enjoy today's letter of love! See you soon!

T – Trust & Treasure

Wednesday, May 11, 2017

Dear Mom –

TGIAF! It's almost Friday! When I think about how long and rough this week has been, it reminds me to be wise in spending my treasure and what I even consider a treasure. I'm grateful to you for teaching me the balance between the pursuit of wealth for tangible accumulation and valuing the treasures of life that money can't buy. You and daddy and God's grace have positioned me to experience the tangible treasures of this life at an early age. Still, you have also helped me understand the pursuit of love, joy, peace, health, and righteousness, a true treasure that exceeds any number of commas.

I've never seen you chase money or misplace the priority of work to where it takes precedence over family time. You've taught me what it means to be ambitious and appropriate, prosperous and purposeful, successful and sacrificial, better and balanced, professional, and

Girls Trip to Maui

present. You were always there. You put us before your career. You ensured we always had the absolute best. You made every practice, scrimmage, game, rehearsal, and meet. You even took our friends home afterward. You said no, so we could say yes, and I am so grateful for every sacrifice you have made to ensure that we always knew where your treasure was.

It's been a blessing to watch you give. From giving family and friends clothes to places to stay to cars and everything in between. My prayer is that I will adequately prioritize the treasure God places in my possession and utilize the provision He blesses me with to be a blessing to others like you have been to so many.

There is no way to give the way I've watched you and daddy give to others without trusting that God is faithful to His promises. Sometimes we place trust in the pseudo security of money, only to realize it leaves our hands like sand. However, you've taught me that when we put our trust in the One that provides the money we receive AND maintain an open hand to give that same money freely to others, He will give you more of it! Bryan, Troy, and I have never wanted for anything, and it was never because we were rich but always because you were a good steward of your treasure and trusted in the Source of your supply until He made it a surplus! As long as I live, you and daddy will never want for anything either. Love you!

H – Honesty and Humility

Thursday, May 12, 2017

Dear Mom –

If you can't handle the truth, don't ask you. You're always honest with others about your beliefs, points of view, and feelings... even when they don't conform to popular opinion. I think it takes courage to have that type of approach in all things. I've watched you have crucial conversations that most people would crumble over, but in the end, your relationships are better because of the honesty you live by. People respect what you have to say and seek your advice because they know that the answer they will get will be honesty wrapped in love and humility.

Shopping in Times Square

You've taught me that honesty should be tempered by humility, so people want to hear what you have to say and don't perceive you as a know it all. Your humility allows others to see Christ in your conversation. As John wrote, you decrease so that

Christ will increase and be seen.

Here are some lessons on honesty and humility that I've learned from you:
1. Honesty and humility are vital to conflict resolution.
2. Just because you're honest in sharing your opinion doesn't mean you're right.
3. There's a time and place to share your honesty.
4. Sometimes, unsolicited honesty isn't necessary – you can be right and rude.
5. Making Jesus famous automatically puts us in good standing with the right people.
6. Humility is the result of understanding who God is and who we are in Him – compared to Him, we are all filthy rags.
7. Being true to self doesn't trump The Truth of God's word.

Thank you for all the lessons you've taught us. Love you!

E – Example of excellence

Saturday, May 14, 2017

Dear Mom –

Happy Mother's Day weekend! I'm so grateful to spend another one with you! This is probably the life lesson that I would say is ingrained in my DNA. "If it's worth doing, it's worth doing well. Do it right or don't do it at all." Excellence is an example you shared and showed with us growing up, in everything from your diligence at work to how you served others to the way that you would clean and keep us together. One of the things I love about your example of excellence is that you never expect the results of your excellence to point to you. It's always about God's glory.

Jesus at the center – of even cleaning the house – becomes the reason and result of your excellence. This is a powerful lesson, in my opinion, because I've learned that when He is the motivation, not people, I can't help but strive with all my might for excellence. When the Master is the measure, it minimizes the mindset of mediocrity. I love these verses as a result:

1 Corinthians 10:31 So, whether you eat or drink, or whatever you do, do all to the glory of God

Colossians 3:23-24 Whatever you do, work heartily, as for the Lord and not for men, knowing that from the Lord, you will receive the inheritance as your reward. You are serving the Lord Christ.

Colossians 3:17 And whatever you do, whether in word or deed, do it all in the name of the Lord Jesus, giving thanks to God the Father through him

So regardless of if it takes longer or costs a bit more, it's hard for me to cut corners and not strive to give my best. Thank you for instilling this in me – not just by your words but by your example.

An example. You are a Proverbs 31 example to the utmost. This is the most critical part of motherhood and the piece I pray to one day embody. An example to my children that serves as an illustration, model, or precedent. You told us, and then you showed us. You stopped and sacrificed so we could start and be successful. It was never enough to tell us the way; you made sure we saw you leading the way. I'm not a mother yet, but this is the difference I see in so many – they stop at telling and yelling. Thank you for the live and in living color illustration of an example of excellence.

I hope you enjoy all that this weekend of love will be! Love you always!

First Time Adventures in Maui

R – Respect and Reciprocity

Mother's Day 2017

Dear Mom –

Happy Mother's Day! I hope you have enjoyed this booklet of love letters filled with lessons you've shown me. Every lesson is built on some form of relationship. We are meant to be in relationship with others – from Christ to friendships to marriage to colleagues. I've watched your relationships at each of these levels, and one of the driving forces to them being successful has been respect.

You've taught me that before I can expect people to respect me, I must first respect myself. This is so vitally important in relationships. When I respect myself, I'm aware of my values and don't compromise them for career gain, relational influence, or romantic interest. I remember this lesson so loudly as it related to dating – when men see that you respect yourself, which means you have boundaries, they have only two choices: respect you or roll on. This lesson did most of the surface hard work for me during my dating years because it would automatically eliminate dead beats on sight, lol! Thanks, mom! In all of my mentoring of young girls from Nashville to Columbia to Knoxville to Chattanooga, this is the lesson I always try to leave with them that you've taught me – respect yourself, and others will mirror back that level of respect for you. ☺

Once I was in a relationship of mutual respect, then I was able to lean on this last lesson of reciprocity. Respect and reciprocity are indeed the recipes for remaining in a relationship.

Reciprocity can be hard at times, but it gives L.I.F.E. to our relationships if we remember that reciprocity requires:

L.ISTENING: Most people say that communication is the key to relationships. While I agree, I would go a bit deeper and say that listening sustains relationships. We often associate communication with initiating or engaging in conversation, but what I've learned is that our loved ones are often communicating (verbally and non-verbally), but we aren't listening. Reciprocity requires active listening to truly hear and understand so that you can mirror back what's being given out.

I.NTERDEPENCE: You've taught me to be a wise, strong, and kindhearted woman that is capable of being independent but able to be interdependent. This protected me from unbalanced and unhealthy relationships of co-dependency. In interdependent relationships, both people are strong and maintain their values and uniqueness while also respecting and nurturing the other's wants and needs. There is no misplaced weight of "completion" created by the other, but rather two complete in Christ individuals come together to complement one another.

F.ORGIVENESS: Oooh wee, this is the big one! Lol! There is no reciprocity without forgiveness daily. I've learned that having the heart to forgive without rehearsing the other person's wrongs allows me to be able to reciprocate the goodness and mercy that Christ gives to us. This aspect of reciprocity exposes our level of faith in Christ because this runs counter to our natural predisposition. The flesh wants to get back, and His Spirit in us propels us to forgive.

E.MPATHY: Empathy is the last requirement of reciprocity that gives L.I.F.E. to our relationships. Empathy is very dependent on listening to understand and then share in the feelings of the other person. You and daddy have been married for a long time, and I've heard and watched empathy in our home growing up. Empathy requires compassion, practicing acts of kindness, undivided attention, listening, and love!

I pray that I can share these lessons that you've taught me with other people and, most importantly, that I live these lessons each day. Hopefully, these open letters have inspired others to take hold of these 6 (really 12 ☺) pearls of wisdom not only to look good but to, most of all, LIVE BETTER!

Mom, I LOVE YOU, and I'm so grateful to spend Mother's Day 2017 together! God is so good, and I am thankful!

Welcome to Las Vegas!

> **ARE YOU READY TO**
> Own Your Brilliance
> Own Your Career
> Own Your Development

SCHEDULE YOUR CONSULTATION

BRITTANYNCOLE.COM → COACHING

✉ BRITTANY@CAREERTHRIVERS.COM

in LINKEDIN.COM/IN/BRITTANYNCOLE

◎ INSTAGRAM.COM/BRITTANYNCOLE

PERSONAL BRANDING & INCLUSIVE LEADERSHIP COACH
Keynote Speaker | Author | CEO

Brittany N. Cole

PERSONAL BRANDING & INCLUSIVE LEADERSHIP COACH

Keynote Speaker | Author | CEO

SPEAKING TOPICS INCLUDE

RESILIENT LEADERSHIP:
THRIVING THROUGH CHANGE

PERSONAL BRANDING & EXECUTIVE PRESENCE:
THE ART AND IMPACT OF INTRODUCING YOUR VALUE

BEYOND DIVERSITY:
  LEADING WITH EMPATHY & INCLUSION
  Inclusive Leadership behaviors for cultivating a culture of belonging

  THE AWARENESS AND ACTIONS OF ALLIES®
  Allyship and gender equity

FOR VIDEO OR MORE INFO TO INVITE BRITTANY TO SPEAK AT YOUR NEXT EVENT, PLEASE VISIT **BRITTANYNCOLE.COM/SPEAKER**

METRO NASHVILLE PUBLIC SCHOOLS | THE UNIVERSITY OF TENNESSEE KNOXVILLE | HARVARD Kennedy School

ENCOURAGING & EQUIPPING LEADERS TO *Thrive*

Brittany N. Cole

PERSONAL BRANDING & INCLUSIVE LEADERSHIP COACH

Keynote Speaker | Author | CEO

"Brittany spoke on Diversity, Inclusion, and Equity at our industry conference and came with knowledge, experience, and engagement. In the lead up to the event, she took the time to learn about our organization and then crafted her talk from there. *I cannot recommend her enough!*"
- ROBYN, VICE PRESIDENT

"*Brittany lead a fantastic session today - the best one I've attended* (including when I was the speaker.) It was informative and more importantly very clear and concise on practical steps to improve."
- CRAIG, PRESIDENT

"I have seen numerous people raving about her message, "Redefining Resilience to Cultivate an Inclusive Culture." *Brittany is a shining star in our community,* and I will not hesitate to recommend her for every speaking opportunity that comes up because I feel her expertise and authenticity can benefit any and all audiences."
- ALLISON, TEDX ORGANIZER

FOR VIDEO OR MORE INFO TO INVITE BRITTANY TO SPEAK AT YOUR NEXT EVENT, PLEASE VISIT **BRITTANYNCOLE.COM/-SPEAKER**

BRITTANY@CAREERTHRIVERS.COM | LINKEDIN.COM/IN/BRITTANYNCOLE | INSTAGRAM.COM/BRITTANYNCOLE

CAREER THRIVERS PODCAST

Thrive through transitions with authenticity, purpose, courage, and joy each week with Brittany and special guests!

Listen on Apple Podcasts
Listen on Google Podcasts
Spotify

SUBSCRIBE TO THE CAREER THRIVERS PODCAST ON APPLE, GOOGLE OR SPOTIFY OR VISIT BRITTANYNCOLE.COM/PODCAST

CAREER THRIVERS®

THE AWARENESS + ACTIONS OF
Allies®

COMBINING CHALLENGING CONVERSATIONS WITH CLEAR ACTION TO CULTIVATE AN INCLUSIVE CULTURE WHERE EVERYONE BELIEVES THEY BELONG.

LIVE Training
Our team partners with your organization to deliver this training LIVE virtually and/or in person

DIGITAL Course
We help you deliver this training online via 7 modules of on demand course content

CUSTOM Content
We add your branding or even your leaders for our white label customization of this training

---

Flexible formats to meet the needs of your team
Building awareness and actionable learning to cultivate an inclusive culture

WWW.CAREERTHRIVERS.COM | INFO@CAREERTHRIVERS.COM | BRITTANY COLE, CEO

CAREER THRIVERS

THE AWARENESS + ACTIONS OF
Allies®
THE DIGITAL COURSE

Interactive Course Modules Include:

Awareness
Agile Emotional Intelligence Assessment

Learning
Cross-cultural resource deep dive

Listening
Strategies for active listening and belonging

Inclusion
Intentional actions to include difference

Experiences
Exposure to the breadth of cross-cultural communities

Sponsorship
Strategies for advocacy of diverse talent

WWW.CAREERTHRIVERS.COM | INFO@CAREERTHRIVERS.COM | BRITTANY COLE, CEO

CPSIA information can be obtained
at www.ICGtesting.com
Printed in the USA
LVHW092119160221
679322LV00017B/801/J